# THE COMPLETE KIT HOUSE CATALOG

Most Pocket Books are available at special quantity discounts for bulk purchases for sales promotions, premiums or fund raising. Special books or book excerpts can also be created to fit specific needs.

For details write the office of the Vice President of Special Markets, Pocket Books, 1230 Avenue of the Americas, New York, New York 10020.

# THE COMPLETE KIT HOUSE CATALOG

### BY

### FRANK COFFEE

PUBLISHED BY POCKET BOOKS NEW YORK

POCKET BOOKS, a division of Simon & Schuster, Inc.
1230 Avenue of the Americas, New York, N.Y. 10020

Copyright © 1979 by Frank K. Coffee

All rights reserved, including the right to reproduce
this book or portions thereof in any form whatsoever.
For information address Pocket Books, 1230 Avenue
of the Americas, New York, N.Y. 10020

ISBN: 0-671-60716-2

First Pocket Books printing June, 1985

10 9 8 7 6 5

POCKET and colophon are registered trademarks
of Simon & Schuster, Inc.

Printed in the U.S.A.

# Contents

| | |
|---|---|
| Introduction | 7 |
| Log Houses | 11 |
| Dome Homes | 47 |
| A-Frames | 67 |
| Chalets | 77 |
| Polygons and Round Houses | 89 |
| Traditionals | 107 |
| Contemporaries | 125 |
| Hideaways and Starters | 141 |
| Solar Houses | 148 |
| Getting Started | 156 |
| Water Supply | 159 |
| Sewage Disposal | 161 |
| Electric System | 163 |
| Heating | 165 |
| Financing Kit Houses | 169 |
| Directory of Manufacturers | 172 |
| Quick Indexes | 176 |

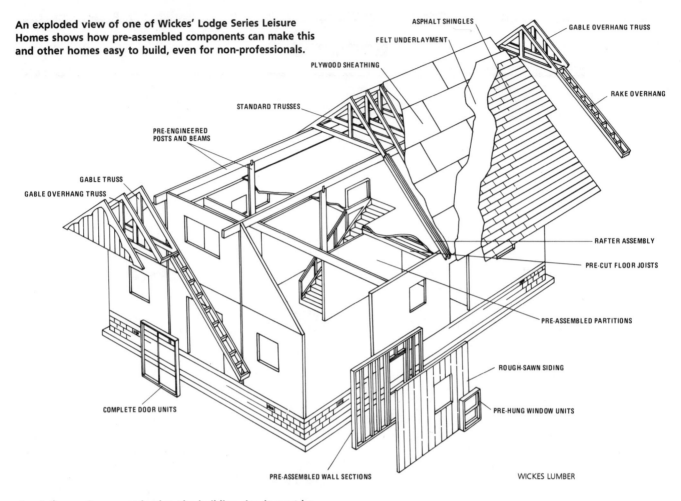

An exploded view of one of Wickes' Lodge Series Leisure Homes shows how pre-assembled components can make this and other homes easy to build, even for non-professionals.

For delivery of a pre-cut load to the building site, it must be accessible for a 65-foot rig carrying up to 40,000 pounds.

# Introduction

Owning a detached single-family home with all the comforts has long been an integral part of the American Dream. It's also the best hedge against inflation. The house built today almost certainly will be worth more tomorrow. But how can you fulfill that dream—and at the same time begin building equity—if the median price of a new site-built house keeps climbing faster than your income, and, as is the case with a staggering number of families today, especially younger ones, you can't qualify as a would-be buyer?

Don't abandon the dream. There's a way of rolling back housing prices. It's called "sweat equity." A fine old American tradition, sweat equity is spending—or investing—your own energy instead of cash. To acquire the house they want but can't afford, more and more families, after looking at the other alternatives, are building at least part of their new home themselves, for very real dollar savings.

It wasn't too long ago that most family men who ventured beyond the eastern metropolises knew at least the fundamentals of carpentry and could give a good account of themselves at a barn raising or even construct their own home. So don't think that just because you don't know the difference between a crosscut and a rip saw you are disqualified from even thinking about raising a roof over your head. If you can drive a nail without whacking your thumb, and have the time and patience, you can build a house—not necessarily from scratch with stock lumber, but one that comes in kit form, either as prebuilt panels or with all the lumber pre-cut and numbered to correspond to its exact location in the plan.

The concept of the packaged house is not new. Back in 1624, a two-story prefabricated dwelling was brought to these shores from England and erected at Cape Ann, Massachusetts. During the Civil War years, structures prebuilt for assembly on temporary or permanent sites were widely used. And lest you think that the owner-built pre-cut that can be ordered by mail is a recent phenomenon, between 1906 and 1937, nearly 100,000 pre-cut houses were sold through the Sears, Roebuck catalog.

The Sears program fell victim to the Depression. But following World War II, factory construction techniques played a large role in meeting the demand not only for primary houses, but for secondary homes for leisure use, as well. With a seller's market, most pre-cuts and prefabs packaged for the owner-builder were cottages, cabins, and unimaginative structures that did little to advance the industry's image. It was catch-up housing and looked it. About the only lasting thing to have come out of that post-war period was the now well-established A-frame.

Times and designs have changed. Today, kit houses come in every size and shape imaginable—from the time-tested log cabin to prestigious suburban residences designed by leading architects. If a kit manufacturer doesn't have quite what you have in mind, most are

**American Pioneer Buildings' two-bedroom Michigan model goes up fast. This is the third day of construction—and the loft and partitions are already installed. The basic shell kit, plus deck, partitions, loft, and stairs, costs around $10,000.**

Construction of a Pacific Panel home is speeded with wall and window panels that come complete with studs, plates, and exterior wall.

prepared to custom-cut it for you. The pre-cutting operation consists of cutting studs, joists, and other structural components—the basic framing elements of the house—to a specified size and notching and pre-drilling them for easy assembly. Each precision-cut piece is then numbered for location within the overall plan and packed in sequence for delivery to the construction site. Eliminated is the costly and time-consuming measuring and cutting of lumber at the site.

With most construction problems worked out in advance in a controlled factory environment, your house grows from foundation to roof quickly and easily, saving you the cost and delays of expensive on-site labor and wasted material. Weather problems and pilferage are virtually eliminated, as most kit houses can be "dried in"—with walls, roof, and lockable doors and windows in place—in far less time than it takes with conventional stick-built construction.

With a panelized house, even more of the work is done in the factory. Making the most of efficient in-plant equipment and building techniques that machines can perform more perfectly than man, walls are delivered to the site in ready-to-be-erected sections, usually with doors and windows installed. Major builders such as Kingsberry Homes have advanced the state of the art to the point where a seven-man Kingsberry crew can put a good-size, largely panelized house together on a previously prepared foundation in two eight-hour days. The exactness that is achieved is all but impossible in conventional on-site construction, and you've got a closed-in house ready for wiring, plumbing, heating, and painting in any kind of weather.

While the shells of most packaged houses go up quickly, the finishing details, from shingles to interior trim, can take just as much time as is required with conventional construction. You're going to have to decide early on not just how much you can do yourself, but how much you *want* to do yourself. This will depend to a large extent on: 1) how much time you have at your disposal; and 2) your budget. But you've also got to be realistic about your abilities and the patience required with a project as formidable as building a house. If you have construction experience as a do-it-yourselfer, you'll find that most of the work takes more time than talent. Outside help is most often needed—and may be required, depending on local building codes—to lay the foundation, install a fireplace and chimney, bring in electricity, and add plumbing and heating.

Roughly 22 percent of the 1,500,000 single-family houses that will be built this year, including log houses, vacation homes, and such construction hybrids as domes, will be based on pre-cut and assembly oriented systems. This doesn't mean, however, that 330,000 of us will be hammering together our own homes. The buyer of a pre-cut or prefab doesn't always have the option of building his house himself. Some of the biggest prefabricators deal only with professional builders. Others discourage owner participation until somewhere between the dried-in and turn-key stages.

But that's fine if you don't wish to tackle the "heavy" work, which is the case with about half of those who participate in the building of their own home. Erected by an experienced crew, the shell of a pre-cut or prefab can still represent a savings of 10 percent or better over conventional construction. With the shell erected by others, the project isn't nearly so terrifying to the novice, and it's an increasingly popular builder/homeowner arrangement, with the homeowner completing the interior in his own good time.

Even if you turn the entire project over to a general contractor, you'll still save money with most kits—not nearly as much, however, as you will by doing as much of the work as you can yourself or acting as your own general contractor. Being your own general contractor, making your own arrangements with plumbers, electricians, and the like, can save 10 to 20 percent in construction costs. Eliminate most labor costs *and* contractor profits and the dedicated do-it-yourselfer can save from 20 to 35 percent of what the completed house would cost if he paid others to do all the work. A $30,000 investment can easily result in a house that is appraised at $45,000. The balance is sweat equity.

As you explore this book, you will find there are packaged houses for every budget and of almost every conceivable design—ranging from compact vacation homes that cost under $5,000 and that you can easily put up yourself, to multi-level suburban residences that can cost $50,000 and up and for which you'll likely need more than a little help. With individual manufacturers offering as many as 170 different models, plus custom treatments, you shouldn't miss not having the house designed expressly for you—especially when you're spared an architect's fee, which is normally 10 to 15 percent of the total construction cost. If we were to attempt to include photographs and specifics on every model offered by every manufacturer of kit houses, we'd need more pages than there are in the Sears catalog.

While bankers hold that the prospective home buyer can't afford a house that costs more than from two to two and one half times his annual income, there's no rule of thumb that relates the cost of a kit to the cost of the completed house. No two manufacturers package alike. Kit prices can represent anywhere from 15 to 75 percent of the cost of the house, excluding the cost of the land and site improvements.

Some kits are complete down to kitchen cabinets and coat hooks. Others include only those materials needed to complete the outer walls. Very few include plumbing, electric, and heating systems. The limited package makes sense, however, when the customer can just as easily buy his dimensional lumber, sheathing, shingles, insulation, paint, and other standard materials from local suppliers. He not only saves shipping charges, but has wider selections from which to choose.

There are manufacturers who will deliver the makings of a house to any part of the country, or the world, for that matter. But you can lose some of the advantages of kit-building if you have to bring up to 40 tons of pre-cut materials halfway across the country. We would try to avoid disproportionately large shipping charges. If we were planning to build a log house in upstate New York, we wouldn't order our logs from a mill in the Pacific Northwest—not when there are a dozen or more log manufacturers in the New York-New England area.

Except with the geodesic dome, framing systems for which can be shipped from coast to coast for under $500, the normal shipping radius for many kit manufacturers is about 350 miles. Flatbed trailers, at between $1.00 and $1.50 a mile per trailer (with most houses you need two), are generally used for deliveries under 800 miles. Beyond that, it's usually cheaper to ship by rail.

There are more than 150 companies in this built-by-the-numbers field. Some have factories in several states so that almost every area of the country can be served. Others operate only east or west of the Mississippi. There also are companies that serve just a small locale. And new companies are coming into the industry almost every month. For that reason, after you've read through this book, check the Yellow Pages of your telephone directory, or those of the nearest big cities, for listings under "Buildings—Pre-Cut, Prefabricated." There might be a resident kit-house company not mentioned in these pages. It's quite possible, too, that some of the manufacturers reviewed will have local representation and perhaps even a model home convenient for your inspection.

We've provided some quick indexes to help you find what you're seeking (i.e., compact vacation homes, domes, log houses, traditional designs, etc.). Using the addresses provided in the back of the book, write to those manufacturers whose designs interest you, starting with companies that either market nationally or have a factory within a few hundred miles of your building site. As noted, many of these companies offer plans books and full-color catalogs for which there is a charge. But this detailed material will be most useful in helping you arrive at your ultimate home-buying or building decision.

In pinning down details, we've included many kit prices. We would hope for the best, but with inflation threatening to become as permanent as taxes, there undoubtedly will be increases in more than a few of these prices between the writing of this book and your reading it.

We are particularly grateful to the many manufacturers who supplied photographs and artwork so that we could bring to the reader the broadest possible coverage of kit-built houses today.

**Even with the time saved with pre-cut and panelized parts, with many kit houses it can still take months of hard work before you're ready to add the final finishing touch to your new home.**

The solid realities of yesterday are wedded to the dreams of today—and tomorrow—in this Rustic Log Structures home built of precision-notched, hand-peeled ledgepole pine logs.

# LOG HOUSES

What man or boy hasn't dreamed at one time or another of going off into the wilds and building a log cabin, just as Dan'l Boone did? Though the techniques of log building were practiced in Scandinavia long before the Pilgrims landed, log cabins are a revered part of this nation's heritage. But a home built of logs today isn't necessarily a log cabin.

While there are those rugged individualists who still insist on hewing their own timber and building a chinked cabin in the frontier style, most of the more than 24,000 log houses that will be erected this year will be put together from logs as uniformly milled as the Lincoln Logs of childhood. With the log-cabin renaissance, more than 40 companies offer pre-cut log-home kits for constructing everything from simple one-room hunting cabins and weekend retreats to ranch, two-story, and split-level models designed to be used as primary residences. Log houses today are no more out of place in a suburban subdivision than they are nestled in the deep woods or on the shore of a favorite lake.

This type of construction has much in its favor. For many, it satisfies the desire to get back to the basics and have a closer harmony with nature. Log houses also can be incredibly durable, and unlike the typical tract house, they have character. Even without braided rugs and stone fireplaces, they have a unique down-home warmth.

Among the natural advantages, solid wall logs (and hollow ones, too) provide one of the most efficient insulating materials known. They can contribute to energy savings of up to 35 percent over conventional FHA stud-wall construction. Tightly constructed log houses are cool in summer, easy to heat in winter. Additional insulation usually is not necessary except in the roof area, and then only in regions of the country where temperatures are extreme. If you plan to build in snow country, look for manufacturers whose designs feature double-insulated-roof construction.

There's not much difference in cost between conventional and log house building materials. However, substantial savings are possible with log construction,

**Log house built in Juneau, Alaska, from a Rustic Log Structures kit**

**The Broken Arrow, by Beaver Log Homes, can be constructed with 864 or 1,032 square feet plus a 384-square-foot loft. With Beaver Log's system of construction, the walls of either version can be completely assembled in less than 48 man-hours.**

A "natural" alternative to conventional housing near the city, Boyne Falls' northern white cedar Salt-Box complements today's informal, energy-conscious life-styles. This Early American design includes four upstairs bedrooms and is located in a subdivision.

You are the judge as to your ability to construct a pre-cut log home. But if you have some carpentry expertise or are handy with tools, the modest two-bedroom Berkshire I, by New England Log Homes, should be within the capabilities of a couple or a growing family looking to enjoy the creative experience of building their own home.

Built of northern white cedar, Boyne Falls' Centennial log home is based on a design that has been popular from the Gulf of Mexico to northern Canada for more than 200 years. The Centennial has functional design, easy maintenance, and excellent insulating qualities right for any climate. The lower floor includes one bedroom, and there is a loft that can provide sleeping space or be finished off into additional bedrooms.

A typical crawl-space foundation with concrete-block walls

Preparing the foundation is almost always the responsibility of the owner where a kit house is involved. It should be completed well before the kit arrives.

especially if you erect the log walls yourself. With the logs serving as exterior siding, sheathing, framing, insulation, and finished inside wall in one, construction not only is speeded but greatly simplified. You don't need a gang of high-priced carpenters to lay up log walls—not when the logs have been precisely milled, pre-cut, and code-numbered for their exact location in the structure.

Some kit mills turn out logs that have been planed flat and V-matched to give the appearance of paneling on the inside wall. Others simply peel the logs for a natural look. To cover up or disguise these walls, which may be waxed, stained, oiled, or varnished, would be self-defeating. The beauty of the wood is lasting and calls for only minimum maintenance. A light sanding will usually remove any dirt that gets into the logs during construction.

Northern white cedar and pine are the kinds of woods used most frequently in log house building today. Northern white cedar is one of the lightest and strongest of North American woods. It is naturally insect and rot resistant. Over the years, it weathers to a soft, silver gray. The species of pine most frequently used are lodgepole, eastern white, plantation, and ponderosa. With these durable softwoods, most pre-cut wall logs will weigh less than 100 pounds.

It is normal for any large, solid timber to develop checks and cracks as it ages, unless a deep kerf has been sawn after debarking to promote more even drying and seasoning. This scarring, however, will not endanger the structural integrity of the building and, in overhead beams especially, contributes to the Early American flavor.

You might think that a log is a log is a log. But the logs that make up the outer walls of a kit-built house come in many proprietary shapes. However, whether turned to an unnatural roundness on a lathe or flatted on two sides or more, most wall logs are milled for tongue-and-groove or spline assembly. A few manufacturers simply plane their logs to a uniform thickness. By using continuous-strip polyurethane gasketing for a weather-tight seal, the interface fit, with virtually every log variation, is so snug that little or no old-style caulking is required.

Not all manufacturers notch their corner logs, but when they do, the interlocking corners, coupled with tongue-and-groove assembly, often makes for such a solid structure that no additional fastenings are necessary. The majority of systems, though, call for each log course to be secured to the one below, using staggered spikes or hidden bolts.

Horizontal-log construction eliminates all vertical framing and is more common than vertical-log or stockade construction. But vertical-log construction has some advantages, as does mixed horizontal and vertical construction. For one thing, horizontal logs, of necessity, are heavier—and more costly—than vertical logs. With vertical logs, there is no settling of walls from shrinkage, there are no complex corner joints, and there's instant runoff of water. With horizontal logs, unless milled to ensure a uniformly engineered wall, trapped water can be a problem. Vertical construction also allows the use of shorter logs (under 8 feet), half-logs, and panelized wall sections.

Log packagers generally offer a variety of plans—from tidy weekenders with a bunkroom to five-bedroom designs with attached garages. Virtually every manufacturer will work with the customer and tailor a plan to suit his special requirements. Costs of the log-home kits vary as widely as do the designs, as will be seen in the following pages. But note that some companies supply a virtually complete package of construction materials. Others supply only the seasoned logs and those materials needed to complete the outer walls of the house. The items most often excluded are flooring, roofing materials, stairs, and partitioning. This makes sense when you can purchase dimensional lumber, sheathing, and shingles locally, from a much wider selection, and avoid additional transportation charges. This applies also, of course, to wiring, plumbing, heating, and masonry. And what's a log home without a fireplace and chimney?

The buyer of a log-house package usually has three options: 1) he can undertake to build the house himself; 2) he can have the shell erected by a crew provided by the manufacturer or dealer; or 3) he can turn the job over to a contractor. While many will undertake to do most of the construction work themselves, nearly as many choose to have others handle the job through the roofed-in shell stage. With log houses, however, less than 10 percent elect to have all the work, including the interior details, done by professionals.

If you do most of the construction work yourself, figure roughly two and one half to three times the cost of the basic pre-cut kit as the complete cost of the house, exclusive of land. By doing the bulk of the labor themselves, do-it-yourselfers build in an equity of as high as 35 percent by the time they put the finishing touches on their house. Built by a contractor, the cost of a log house is usually about 10 percent less than that of a conventional site-built house with the same features.

With the revival of interest in log houses, most kit manufacturers are backlogged for months. When you order a log house, don't expect delivery of the kit to coincide with an early vacation. You may have to give the producer up to 12 months notice if you want delivery during the summer months.

You can go ahead though and study the working drawings and the manufacturer's construction guide. The foundation also must be prepared well ahead of delivery of the log package. In pioneer days, most log

It generally takes two flatbed trailers, each carrying up to 40,000 pounds, to deliver the makings of a log house to the building site. Unloading is usually the customer's responsibility. All roads leading to the desired unloading site must be accessible for 65-foot rigs.

Log walls are heavy and you need a good foundation, with solid footings below the frost line. Most log houses are built on a continuous-wall foundation, usually with an enclosed crawl space rather than a basement.

Pre-cut log houses could be called the adult version of the Lincoln Logs of childhood. The single-wall log construction provides exterior siding, insulation, and finished inside wall all in one.

Not all log houses are built with horizontal-log construction. Bellaire Log Cabin Manufacturing Company features vertical-log construction with splined, white cedar half-logs. Under construction here is the two-bedroom Antrim, one of Bellaire's most popular designs for resort or year-round living.

cabins were built with a dirt floor, which is why you don't see any of those early cabins around today. Laying logs directly on the ground leads to rapid decay.

Log walls are heavy and you do need a good foundation, with solid footings below the frost line. Most log houses are built on continuous-concrete-wall foundations, usually with an enclosed crawl space rather than a full basement. Piers for a log structure are a bit tricky and generally not recommended for first-timers. Concrete slab-on-grade is not commonly used with log buildings.

The foundation should be completed several weeks before the logs arrive. The concrete needs time to set before you begin stacking the logs. Since delivery of the logs is generally made via 40-foot flatbed trailers, make sure that a truck (the majority of homes are shipped on two trucks) of this size, carrying up to 40,000 pounds of logs and other components, will be able to negotiate the roads and any bridges leading to the building site. Or provide an alternate off-loading spot from where the logs can be brought in later by a smaller truck.

You'll generally need three helpers, or a couple of helpers and a forklift, to unload the trailer. After arrival, the logs, each coded for its exact position in the construction, will have to be sorted. Logs are bundled for the manufacturer's convenience and not the builder's. Dunnage or straw spread on the ground where the logs will be stacked will help to keep the pre-sanded surfaces clean. Windows and doors should be stored off the ground, but not flat.

Before you start setting your log courses, give some thought to how you intend to wire the house. First-course or "A" logs are sometimes pre-channeled to accept electrical conduits and water lines, which later will be concealed behind baseboard or log siding. Channels also can be chiseled alongside doors and windows and concealed by trim. Still another hidden-wire trick is to drill aligned holes vertically through each log so that wiring can be snaked up to a mortised outlet.

With anything larger than a weekend cabin, construction generally calls for a conventional flooring system and studded partitioning. Here, wall switches and outlets in the interior partitions, as well as the plumbing and heating lines, are installed in the same manner as in a conventional frame building. You *could* relocate all switches and junction boxes to the interior partitions.

Two men with average construction skills, plus two helpers, should be able to erect the shell of a medium-size, one-story log house and close it to the weather in five to seven days. But the rule of thumb with most pre-cut log houses, from start to finish, is three-quarters to one man-hour per square foot of floor area.

The floor plans shown on the following pages are only suggestions. Except where a major structural element is involved, inner partitions may be moved or removed at will.

The rustic practicality of log-home living is the dominant theme throughout the interior of this Vermont Log Buildings home.

# Authentic Homes/The Seneca

Unlike the hand-hewn log homes of our forefathers, today's real log houses are precisely cut and finished. Many designs, such as the ranch-style Seneca, make fine primary residences and are giving a new look to suburbia.

One of the most popular models among the 20 different log-house designs developed by Authentic Homes is the six-room Seneca, a one-story, 1,625-square-foot dwelling featuring two wings connected by a front-and-rear-entry divider. One wing contains three bedrooms; the other accommodates living room, dining room, and kitchen.

Authentic selects standing dead lodgepole or ponderosa pine and debarks the logs to remove any insect-harboring cellulose layers. These logs, averaging 8 to 9 inches in diameter, are then cut and planed to a uniform 6-inch vertical height to interface snugly together.

As with most Authentic kits, the Seneca package contains only the exterior wall logs, floor joists, rafters, gasket and caulking materials, and log-locking spikes. The kits are sold through authorized Authentic Homes dealers who ordinarily construct the shell, then subcontract the work of finishing the house—by adding roof, windows, doors, interior walls, plumbing and electrical facilities, according to the customer's specifications. The homeowner can cut costs by finishing all or part of the house himself. For the man with some construction experience, it's not too difficult to assemble an Authentic log home.

Along with the kit, Authentic provides detailed architectural plans for building the shell and adding roofing, heating, electrical, and plumbing systems. Included are lists outlining quantity, specifications, and suppliers for all materials needed to finish the house according to a suggested floor plan, or one customized according to the customer's ideas.

The kit price for the Seneca is $16,080, F.O.B. Laramie, Wyoming. The two-car garage (Pima model; kit price $4,760) can be built as a separate unit or attached, as shown. Price of the completed house will run from three to five times the cost of the Seneca kit, depending on individual tastes, local building costs, and how much of the work the customer can do himself.

Included in the Authentic line are ranch, two-story, and split-level models designed as primary residences, plus smaller chalets and cabins suitable for vacation homes. Plans are available with up to six bedrooms.

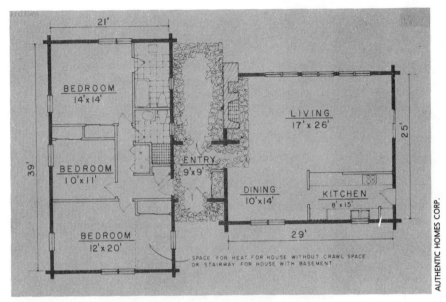

The floor plan of the Seneca shows bedroom and family living wings flanking the enclosed, front-and-rear-access entranceway.

A construction manual guides the builder of an Authentic log home through every stage, from site preparation to interior finishing. The cover of the manual shows another view of the Seneca, the model featured here.

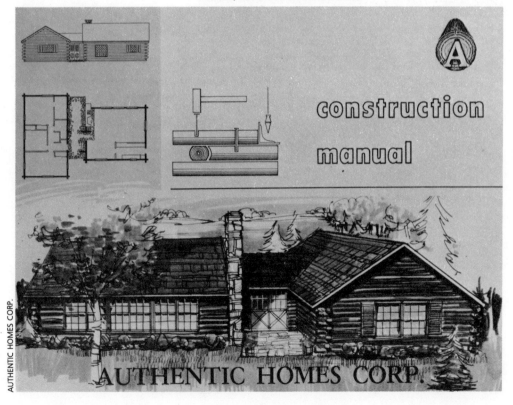

The foundation and sub-floor system should be completed before the arrival of the kit. Finish flooring should not be installed until after the roof has been completed. If the log kit is not scheduled to arrive for some time, cover the sub-floor with plastic.

Authentic Homes' walls are made airtight through the use of urethane foam strips between the planed logs. This snug, permanent form of structural design overcomes the major problems of log systems that use unplaned logs and chinking.

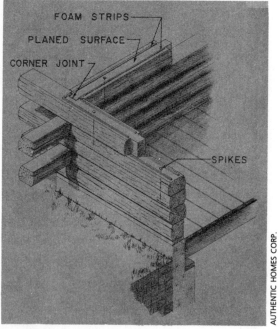

Urethane foam gasket strips between log courses form a tight seal. The gasketing is stapled lightly every three to four feet to anchor the foam until the log above is in position. Staples should run longitudinally with the foam, not across the foam, to avoid creating valleys.

Each pre-cut log is coded according to its position in the building and pre-drilled to mark spike locations. Spikes are driven with a 6- or 8-pound sledge.

Pre-cut log courses go up quickly. Logs are pre-notched at door and window openings to accept frames.

Log rafters are added to complete the shell of the Seneca. Under most circumstances, the roof over an exposed-beam (cathedral) ceiling should be of double construction to provide satisfactory insulation.

# Real Log Homes/The Tyson

The salt-box-styled Tyson is a modest two-bedroom dwelling that could probably be completed by the do-it-yourselfer for under $22,000.

The unpretentious Tyson, with the distinctive lines of an old New England salt-box house, is a versatile structure. Durable and comfortable, it could serve as a hunting or fishing lodge, a vacation home, or as a year-round, permanent abode for a single person or couple. It's also an affordable—and attractive—first home for the young family just entering the housing market. There are two models: the Tyson A, measuring 22 × 34 feet, and the Tyson B, measuring 24 × 46 feet.

The Tyson is one of the more than 30 models offered by Real Log Homes, covering everything from small, cabin-like designs to spacious five- and six-bedroom houses. Styles range from "the olde Kentucky home" to snow-country chalets. Real Log Homes also offers gambrel barn designs and kits for constructing two- and three-car log garages. With manufacturing facilities in Vermont, North Carolina, Montana, and Arkansas, and franchised dealers in over 40 states and Canada, Real Log Homes is the leading producer of log-house kits. Vermont Log Buildings, in Hartland, Vermont, is its principal manufacturer.

Real Log Homes cuts its logs from selected pine logs, 7 to 11 inches thick. The logs are machine de-barked, pre-cut, pre-notched, grooved for spline assembly, and then dipped in a clear, odorless wood preservative to minimize the threat of fungus and insect damage that is inherent in any wood. A periodic re-application of a wood preservative would be one of the few upkeep chores when you live in a Real Log Home.

The Tyson package includes the exterior wall logs, pre-hung windows and doors, ridge pole, rafters and snow blocks, and enough hardboard spline, 10-inch spikes, and PVC gasket material to erect the log structure. Three detailed sets of blueprints, a 32-page construction guide, and at least four hours of on-site technical assistance are also provided. *Not included*:

floor joists and girder, underlayment, finished flooring, conventional interior partitions, insulation, and roof covering.

The finished price for a Real Log Home varies from two and one half times the log-package price for do-it-yourselfers to four to four and one half times the package price for a totally contractor-erected house.

These prices allow for a full basement. Average erection time for a Real Log Homes component package is four to five days for a crew of four men. With the Tyson, it shouldn't take that long, even for relatively inexperienced do-it-yourselfers.

Price for the Tyson A log package is $7,500; for the Tyson B, $9,600.

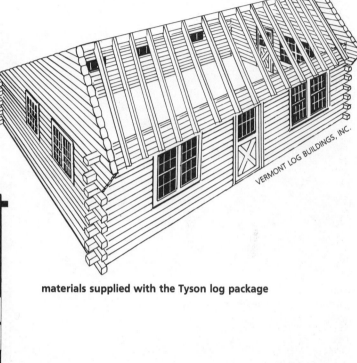

materials supplied with the Tyson log package

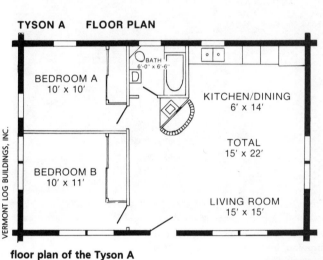

floor plan of the Tyson A

**Stressing the simpler life-style, the atmosphere of a log home like the Tyson, with its natural wood fragrance and quiet mellowness, makes a statement about who you are.**

# Boyne Falls Log Homes/The Virginian

A home built using the rediscovered sill-and-post system of building has more than just construction advantages. The Virginian, by Boyne Falls Log Homes, offers a true alternative to everyday housing, both in appearance and maintenance.

The sill-and-post system of building, used in the 1,456-square-foot, three-bedroom Virginian, by Boyne Falls Log Homes, was popular with French fur trappers and Jesuit missionaries more than 200 years ago. It was also used by Ulysses S. Grant, for his home that still stands at Grant's Farm, St. Louis, Missouri.

This building system takes advantage of the maximum strength of wood, which is with the grain. There are both horizontal and vertical timbers, contributing to exceptional strength in these single-wall-construction log buildings.

Another advantage to the early settlers was that wall sections could be pre-assembled by one man. With horizontally laid timbers supported by vertical log mullions, the cabin walls were then, with a little assistance, easily and quickly erected. The same holds true here. The Boyne Falls sill-and-post building system allows for the home to be pre-cut at the mill and then partially pre-assembled and shipped ready to be erected over basement, crawl space, or any other type of foundation by a Boyne Falls crew, a local contractor, or the homeowner.

The walls (average thickness: 3 1/2 inches) of a Boyne Falls sill-and-post building come 75 percent pre-assembled. The logs are northern white cedar.

Boyne Falls kits include everything needed for the construction of the house, from wall logs and sub-flooring to roof shingles and interior partitions. This is not just a shell. With each log planed flat and milled for a V-joint panel effect on the inside wall, Boyne Falls homes are ready to live in almost as soon as they're up, which can take as little as three weeks.

Price of the sill-and-post Virginian kit: $37,920, F.O.B. Boyne Falls, Michigan. The house can also be built with all vertical logs, for a kit price of $35,690; all horizontal logs, for a kit price of $42,430; or 3 1/2 inch sculptured timber, for a kit price of $37,530.

There are 18 designs in the Boyne Falls portfolio, ranging from cabins to sprawling multi-level houses, most of which can be built with vertical logs, horizontal logs, or sill-and-post construction. Any of these designs can be adapted to suit your needs, whether you live near the city, on a lake in a wooded resort area, or deep in the country.

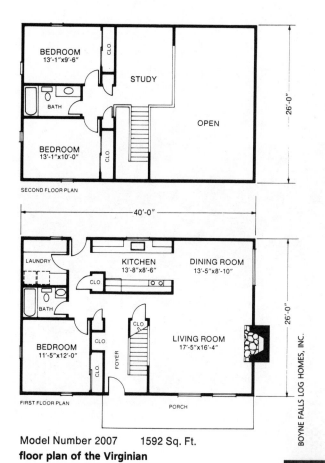

Model Number 2007   1592 Sq. Ft.
**floor plan of the Virginian**

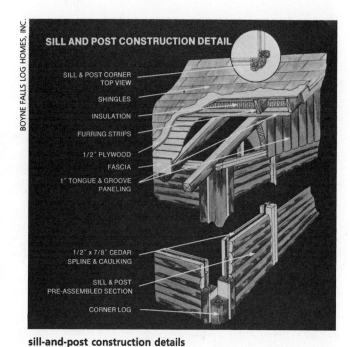

**sill-and-post construction details**

**Over 200 years ago, French trappers built their cabins using the same method of construction that was used to build this Boyne Falls log home. But you can be sure their living rooms never looked like this one. The natural beauty of northern white cedar has been enhanced by the tasteful contemporary furnishings selected by the homeowner.**

# New England Log Homes/The New Englander

The spacious New Englander, with three bedrooms and two baths, is a far cry from the log cabins built in the days of Dan'l Boone and Abe Lincoln.

The New Englander includes 1,504 square feet of floor area on two levels and is one of 30 basic models offered by New England Log Homes, one of the big names in the log-kit industry. As shown in the suggested floor plan, the New Englander easily accommodates three bedrooms and two baths. With the living room open to a cathedral ceiling, the kit price is $15,495. For a full second floor, in lieu of the cathedral ceiling, add $400.

This price covers the pre-cut wall logs, which average 10 inches in diameter; second-floor joists; roof rafters; gable ends; windows; exterior doors; double dormer; porch posts; and enough spline, spikes, gasket material, and caulking compound to assemble the log structure. Roofing and flooring packages can be supplied by New England Log Homes, but generally it's to the customer's advantage to buy decking, sheathing, shingles, and the like locally.

New England Log Homes are constructed from red and white plantation pine logs which have been hand-peeled and planed to provide a flat surface top and bottom before being grooved for splining. In addition, the logs are mortised and tenoned for interlocking corners. As each log course is laid, it is spiked to the one below at 4-foot intervals. For a weathertight seal, hardboard spline is inserted in the groove and continuous PVC gasket is applied on each side of the spline before the next course is seated.

The box-sill has been adopted by New England Log Homes as the most practical method of sill construction. It increases accessibility to the recessed "A" log for installation of electric wiring and baseboard outlets, provides for positive sill anchorage, and allows for the sub-floor and deck to be installed before the log package arrives.

Other models offered by New England Log Homes, which has dealers in 25 states, range from the 704-square-foot Lenox to the 2,880-square-foot Americana; kit prices, from $6,395 to $25,436. In addition to the structural components, the package price includes three sets of blueprints, a builder's manual, and four hours of technical assistance. Prices are F.O.B. Great Barrington, Massachusetts; Houston, Missouri; and Lawrenceville, Virginia. Customers have the option of picking up their log packages at the plant or having New England Log Homes make the delivery. Most of these homes require two 40-foot flatbed trailers to deliver the load.

It takes an experienced crew of three—one carpenter and two aides—approximately two weeks to properly erect the log package for a home the size of the New Englander. Some 47 percent of New England Log Homes' customers elect to leave this much of the construction, through the shell stage, to the professionals. But just as many tackle the entire job themselves, starting with log one. There's another 6 percent who choose not to participate at all in the construction of their home.

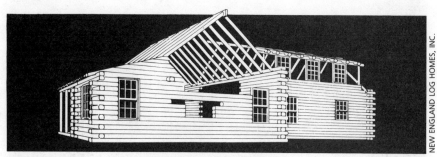

materials supplied with the New Englander log package

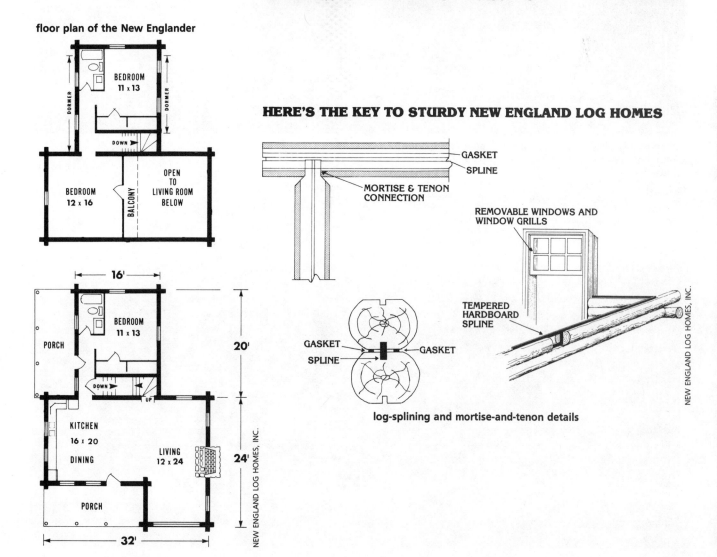

floor plan of the New Englander

**HERE'S THE KEY TO STURDY NEW ENGLAND LOG HOMES**

log-splining and mortise-and-tenon details

Hand-peeled plantation pine logs contribute to the pronounced personality of every New England Log Homes house.

28

# Rustic Log Structures/The Chieftain

Built from hand-peeled lodgepole pine logs and with interlocking crossover corners, the 1,350-square-foot Chieftain has the sort of styling that would make it at home from Big Sur to the Swiss Alps.

Hand-peeled, solid lodgepole pine logs averaging 8 to 10 inches in diameter are the "trademark" of Rustic Log Structures. Retaining their authentic warm character, rather than a manufactured look, logs from this Pacific Northwest mill have been used in the building of nearly 1,000 year-round houses and commercial structures in the Pacific Northwest, across Alaska, into California, and even Japan.

Rustic Log Structures has built lodges with over 9,000 square feet of floor space and can furnish a pre-cut log package for almost any house design. The company has 10 "stock" models, ranging in floor area from 1,008 to 2,852 square feet, but believes each home should be a reflection of the owner. Some 90 percent of the houses it has produced have been custom-cut—either as an adaptation of one of its designs or a design created to meet the customer's special needs.

The hand-peeling of the logs, which are flatted top and bottom for a close-tolerance, minimum-5-inch-wide fit, is done with an old-fashioned draw blade. To be authentic and structurally rigid, the logs are precision notched for interlocking crossover corners.

Rustic Log Structures' attention to detail is reflected in the Chieftain, the model featured here. From the pitch of the roof and the protective overhang to the massive fireplace and the lofty living room ceiling, the 1,350-

square-foot Chieftain has the sort of styling that would make it at home from Big Sur to the Swiss Alps. The design easily allows for three bedrooms, and many have been built with daylight basements. The Chief of the Quinault Indian tribe, appropriately enough, built a Chieftain (what else!) overlooking the Pacific at Taholah, Washington.

The log package for the Chieftain weighs approximately 38,000 pounds and costs $11,700, F.O.B. Ellensburg, Washington. You can order just the logs, a finished home built by professionals on your site, or any stage in between from Rustic Log Structures. This is a matter of your time, talents, and finances.

floor plan of the Chieftain

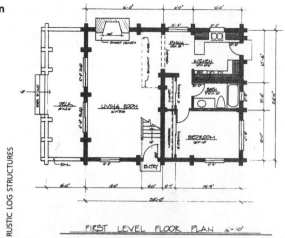
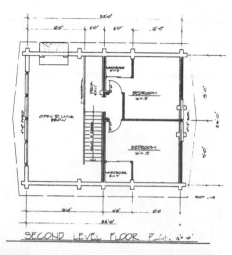

The log package for a Rustic Log Structures home is delivered to the site in 4,000-pound bundles. It helps if you have a forklift available for the off-loading.

Second-level floor beams are being set. All logs are flatted top and bottom to the same vertical dimension and hand-peeled with an old-fashioned draw blade to achieve the desired authentic look.

As one worker installs gasketing, another drills holes to facilitate later installation of electrical outlets and in-the-wall wiring. The sledges are used to seat the interlocking crossover corners, which are precision-notched for a tight fit.

Protective overhangs and the steeper pitch of a Real Log Structures roof are not just architectural whims. Designed for erection primarily in the Pacific Northwest, these houses have to cope with extra-heavy snowfalls.

# National Log Construction/Plan AL47

This comfortable, modern ranch home, with the charm of pioneer days and ways, is one of National Log Construction's most popular designs. Like all National Log homes, it is built with logs that have been hollowed.

There's only one company we know of, at least among U.S. manufacturers, that hollows its logs. That's National Log Construction Company. According to National Log, by boring a sizable hole through, or nearly through, the center of each log (corner logs have a solid end), its Air-Lock Logs not only are lighter in weight for easier handling, but with simultaneous drying from both the inside and outside of the log, checking and cracking are minimized. The hollowed logs also give the builder convenient conduits through which to run wiring.

National Log is one of the oldest manufacturers of pre-cut log houses in the U.S. and has plants in Montana and New Mexico (Air-Lock Log Company). Fifty-five plans, for everything from one-room cabins to modern luxury homes with nearly 3,000 square feet of living space, are included in National Log's catalog. But the strength of this company's business is in its custom-design capability, with over 80 percent of the houses it produces cut to the buyer's own plan or a modified version of one of its standard plans.

Take the house featured here. A comfortable, modern ranch home with the charm of rustic construction, it's one of the National Log's most popular designs. The standard, 1,280-square-foot plan allows for a carport. This owner, however, opted for an enclosed two-car garage as an attractive and functional extension of the house.

Air-Lock Logs come in three diameters. Base price for the standard-plan log package (approximate weight: 14 tons) for the house shown is $11,915, F.O.B. Thompson Falls, Montana. That's for 6-inch-diameter logs. Add 10 percent to that price for 7-inch logs and 20 percent for 8-inch logs. Prices are somewhat lower from Air-Lock Log Company, F.O.B. Las Vegas, New Mexico.

There is no loss of insulation qualities in the hollowed lodgepole pine logs. Dead air space is even better insulation than solid wood. The seasoned logs are precisely turned on huge lathes to the diameter specified for the design before being milled for a tongue in the bottom and a groove in the top. Each log is then cut to the exact length required and marked to correspond with the detailed construction plan. To ensure perfect corners, saddles are cut in the corner logs using barrel saws of the same diameter as the log.

The finished cost of an Air-Lock Log house will vary greatly depending on the customer's choice of fixtures, fireplace, type of foundation, etc. Approximately three to four times the cost of the log-and-related-necessities package is a good rule-of-thumb estimate for the completely finished and furnished house.

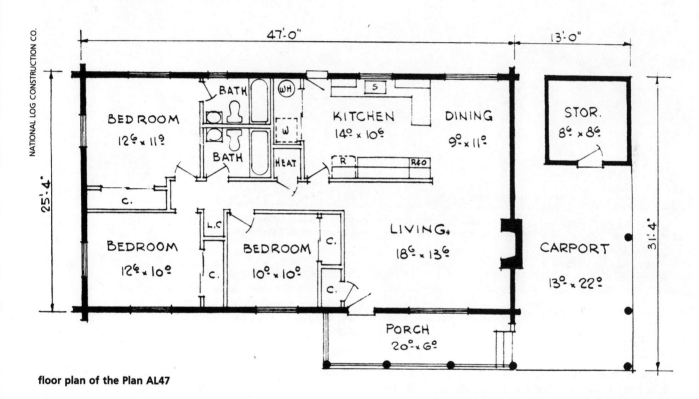

**floor plan of the Plan AL47**

**hollowed Air-Lock logs with tongue-and-groove design**

# Northeastern Log Homes/The Bedford

**Designed for four-season comfort, the four-bedroom Bedford would fit in almost anywhere. It is very adaptable, and a breezeway and garage could easily be added.**

The two-story, four-bedroom Bedford, by Northeastern Log Homes, is a switch on the traditional New England salt-box house. With the long sloping roof facing to the front rather than the rear, this puts fewer restrictions on the orientation of the house and it can fit into almost any setting. There are three upstairs bedrooms, lots of closets, and full baths both upstairs and down. The living room is open to the roof. Including the 6-foot-deep front porch, the floor area of the Bedford totals 1,776 square feet.

Northeastern Log houses are built from 6 × 8-inch eastern white pine logs that have been milled to exact dimensions for tongue-and-groove assembly, with splined butt joints. After the logs are pre-cut to length, numbered and notched for interlocking corners, they are bundled and submerged in a wood preservative to protect against insects and deterioration. The logs are then ready for delivery to the building site via special loader-equipped flatbed trailer trucks.

Price of the pre-cut Bedford kit is $22,485, F.O.B. Groton, Vermont. Northeastern's standard materials package includes logs, windows, doors, floor and roof systems, stair materials, and interior partitioning. The only construction materials not included: roof insulation, nails, and flashing.

Northeastern's solid-log walls and double-insulated roof construction are adaptable to any type of foundation and central heating system and promise a comfortable home in all climates. The company recently added a dozen models to its line and now has a total of 24 log-house designs that offer individuality, durability, and minimum maintenance.

Sales offices are located in Groton, Vermont; Kenduskeag, Maine; and Louisville, Kentucky. You may order any of the standard models exactly as they are designed or make any changes necessary to suit your individual requirements.

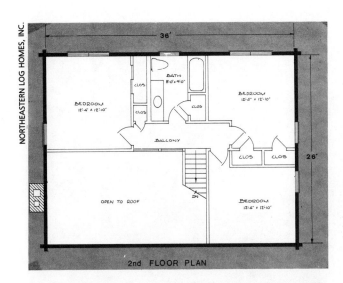

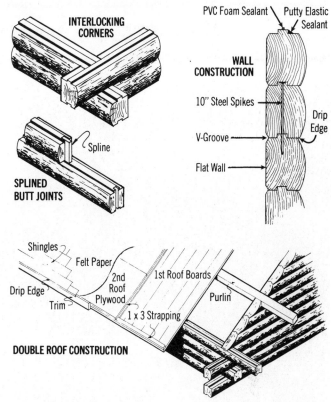

art showing interlocking corners, splined butt joint, and wall and roof construction details

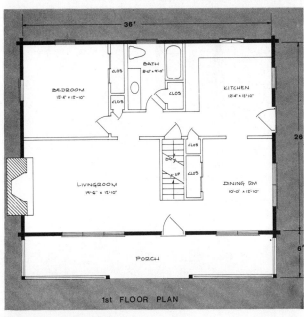

floor plan of the Bedford

**Inside-wall surfaces of Northeastern logs are flatted and V-matched for a pre-finished paneled effect. The walls can be left natural or stained to suit your personal preference.**

# L. C. Andrew/The Killington

Imagine the Killington on a mountain slope ablaze with spring flowers . . . with leaves changing colors in autumn . . . or with the snow quietly sifting down. It has more charm than *The Sound of Music*. Choose a cathedral ceiling over the living, dining, and kitchen area or a full second floor to maximize the living space.

With its rustic charm, the chalet-styled Killington would be out of place on few mountainsides, whether Swiss or domestic. There are two bedrooms, with a cathedral ceiling over the living, dining, and kitchen area, and a large loft for weekend guests. To maximize the functional space in this L. C. Andrew design, you could put in a full second floor.

Unlike most log houses, the Killington features panelized construction. The outer walls are assembled from prefabricated panels with doors and windows installed. Gables also are prefabricated, in sections, and may include a window or a louver. Rather than the traditional single-log wall, the Killington and other L. C. Andrew designs employ northern white cedar log siding backed by 5/16-inch CDX plywood and 15-pound felt paper for airtight and watertight construction. All of the elements are secured to 2 × 4 or 3 × 4 studs, a method of wall construction that also provides for convenience in wiring, plumbing, and insulating. Another plus: you never have to sand, scrape, paint, or varnish cedar siding.

At the mill, each northern white cedar log is peeled and sawn and then milled on three sides with a groove in the bottom and a matching tongue on the top. The logs are next beveled top and bottom to prevent water penetration and to ensure a tight fit. These 3- to 5-inch thick logs are made up into 8-foot-wide panels, with doors and windows (Andersen PermaShield or other windows of your choice) installed as required. The logs are nailed to the studs, through the plywood-and-felt paper liner, with the tongue-and-groove joints pre-caulked to seal out the weather. The panels come to the building site ready to receive the bolts furnished for fastening.

L. C. Andrew prices include all materials necessary to erect the complete exterior shell, including pre-cut rafters, 2 × 6 or 2 × 8 as required; framing material for the floor and interior partitions; one-inch tongue-and-groove pine for the floor and roof sheathing; and self-sealing shingles. Material for the stairs, railing, and upstairs flooring is provided for all models with lofts. Eave and gable trim to match the siding is also included. Interior paneling, insulation materials, screen doors, paint, outside steps, and kitchen cabinets and countertops can be provided as options.

Price of the prefab Killington package, without deck, is $18,972, F.O.B. South Windham, Maine. L. C. Andrew also offers a materials package for the Killington at $16,238. This package includes all the materials mentioned, except that the walls and gables are not prefabricated. Materials packages in this case require complete fitting and erecting on the job.

If you're handy with tools, you may want to gather some friends together and build the Killington or another L. C. Andrew log house on your own. Or you could hire the contractor of your choice. Or have L. C. Andrew recommend a reputable builder who's handled L. C. Andrew "house raisings" before. The company is another that has been in the log-construction business for more than 50 years. Custom design service is offered.

floor plan of the Killington

the snow-covered Killington

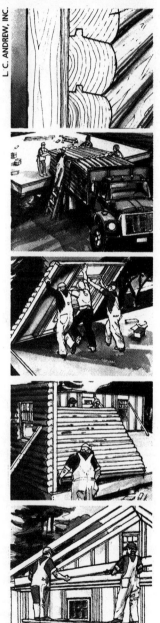

L. C. Andrew system erection details; with the panelized wall system, an average-sized building can be enclosed in a single day by three men.

# Alta Industries/The Altan VI

The techniques of log building were practiced in Scandinavia long before the Pilgrims landed in America, so the much-admired Altan VI, with its distinctive Scandinavian flavor, may be even more "authentic" than most Early American log-house designs.

Hand carvings and wrought-iron exterior hardware are among the finishing touches that give Alta Industries' log houses their distinctive Scandinavian flavor. There's artistry, too, in the double-locking construction. With the logs machined for a perfect fit, each corner interlocks without nailing.

Alta's log houses are constructed from solid white pine logs with horizontal locking grooves in both the top and bottom surfaces to ensure an airtight fit throughout. Butt joints are splined to prevent air passage and little or no caulking is required. With the exterior and interior walls smoothly machined, there are no ledges or mismatched ends to catch rainwater or collect dust.

The Altan VI is one of 26 models offered by Alta—ranging from the 576-square-foot Walton I to the three-bedroom, 1,800-square-foot Woodstock. All of the Alta packages include hand-carved crossbeams and valances for that distinctive Scandinavian look and feeling of comfort for which these houses are noted.

The two-bedroom, 24 × 32-foot Altan VI measures 960 square feet, including an 8 × 24-foot sleeping loft. Price for the shell package, which includes everything except the floor system, roof insulation, and shingles, is $14,820, F.O.B. Halcottsville, New York. For a good line on how much you might save by doing it yourself, Alta's price for a professionally erected Altan VI shell, on your foundation, would be $21,700.

The company has an extensive dealer network, in 18 states, from Maine to Missouri. These dealers are also prepared to build a turn-key Altan VI for you. The price, $31,700, includes excavation for concrete footings and five courses of 8-inch concrete blocks for crawl space, backfilling of disturbed areas, interior partitioning, kitchen cabinets, all plumbing, electrical work, and baseboard electric heating.

another view of the Altan VI, with the sun deck

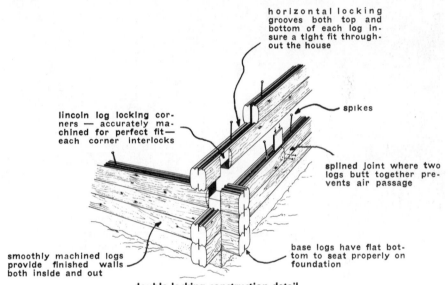

double-locking construction detail

floor plan of the Altan VI

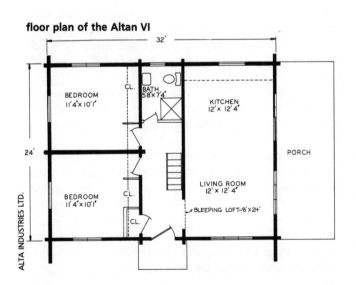

With Alta's double-locking construction, the walls go up quickly and are both solid and airtight. Additional benefits of Alta designs are the smoothly machined interior and exterior walls. There are no ledges or mismatched log ends to trap water or collect dust.

# Ward Cabin/The Laurentide

More than 50 years of experience in log-home manufacturing has gone into Ward Cabin's versatile Laurentide.

Ward Cabin Company has been in the log-manufacturing business for more than 50 years. The experience is reflected in the design of the versatile Laurentide, which could serve equally well as a lakeside cottage, ski chalet, or full-time residence.

The 1,734-square-foot Laurentide includes two bedrooms on the first floor, a 22 × 26-foot sleeping loft over the bedroom and bath areas, and a fully sheltered 10 × 20-foot porch. The living room is open to a cathedral ceiling. Storage is no problem. There are five closets and a utility room on the main floor, in the suggested floor plan.

Ward buildings are designed for erection on any type of foundation. The logs, which are northern white cedar, average 4 1/4 inches in thickness when sawn three sides and milled for tongue-and-groove assembly. With caulking applied between each course and the logs locked together with 8-inch spikes, additional insulation, beyond the natural insulating qualities of the solid cedar logs, is usually not necessary, except in the roof area, and then only if the building is to be used as a year-round residence. All inside wall faces are flat and pre-sanded, with a horizontal V-joint for a paneled effect. A uniform milled exterior is an option, at added cost.

The Ward building system calls for double-roof construction, with strapping applied between the two layers of roof boards, creating an air space for insulation value.

Ward offers "starter," "shell," and "complete" pre-cut log-house packages. The complete kit for the Laurentide, which includes everything in the way of required construction materials except the roof shingles, costs $25,480, F.O.B. Houlton, Maine. The shell price of the Laurentide is $20,470. Price for the starter package, which excludes flooring and roof systems, stair and loft materials, and partitioning, is $17,460.

More than 30 basic log house models are offered by Ward, ranging from the St. Croix, with 660 square feet of floor area, to the 3,700-square-foot Carefree. Ward also offers the Allagash series, with 10 plans, measuring from 20 × 20 to 24 × 42 feet. Utilizing camp-grade logs, which vary in thickness and length and have milling or other imperfections, Allagash shell kit prices range from $5,190 to $13,140.

Ward has authorized sales representatives in most of the Eastern states and some Midwestern states.

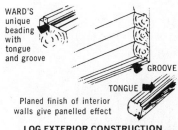

**Ward Cabin construction details**

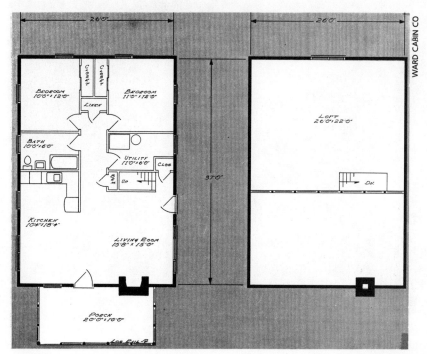

**floor plan of the Laurentide**

The fully-sheltered porch with broken roof line adds function and character to this popular home. The building is designed with an indoor/outdoor fireplace—for cooking outdoors in warm weather, for comfort during the winter months.

# American Pioneer Buildings/The Retreat

With walls prefabricated in sections, floors and roof pre-cut, the Retreat can be erected quickly and easily—with a walk-out basement, as here, or over a crawl space.

The stock designs of most log-kit manufacturers include at least one model with chalet styling. The Retreat, a split-level chalet, is a recent addition to American Pioneer Buildings' line and a good example of panelized, vertical half-log, single-wall construction.

Produced from selected cedar logs cut from the forests of Northern Michigan, the logs are sawn down the middle to make half-logs, which are hand-peeled and thoroughly seasoned before being milled. The seasoned half-logs are dressed for a smooth inside face and grooved deeply to receive the heavy cedar spline used in the rigid-panel assembly.

Before each spline is inserted, a caulking compound is applied to ensure a weathertight seal. Window and door frames are factory installed in wall panels measuring from four to nine feet in width.

For single-wall construction, the inside surface of logs-and-splines forms the inside wall, with a paneled effect. Insulation and double-wall construction, using furring and wallboard or paneling, easily can be added to ensure comfort where winters are severe.

The Retreat model shown here is based on a 27 × 32-foot structure which includes 1,350 square feet of living area. In this case, the basic plan has been extended eight feet, to measure 27 × 40. The basic (27 × 32-foot) shell package, which includes walls, windows, exterior doors, gables, balcony, stairs, and pre-cut roof assembly, costs $14,223, F.O.B. Milford, Virginia. For each additional four feet, add $1,444. This price does not include glass for the front wall.

A feature of American Pioneer Buildings is "water-table" construction, incorporating a specially beveled-and-grooved, 2 × 6 base plate, which drains water away from the walls.

Other models in the American Pioneer line, a number of which are expandable, range from the 320-square-foot Sportsman ($5,369 for the basic shell package) to the 1,204-square-foot Superior ($13,966). Basic deck, partitions-and-trim, and balcony packages are offered as options.

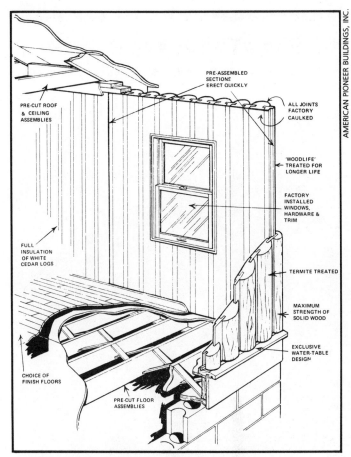

American Pioneer Buildings' construction details

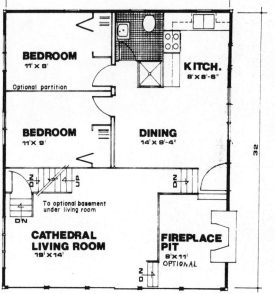

floor plan of the Retreat

No chalet and few log houses are complete without a fireplace. The split-level Retreat can be built with an optional fireplace pit, two steps down from the living room.

The Retreat is a split-level with chalet styling, built with pre-assembled vertical half-log wall sections. Windows and door frames are factory-installed for easy site erection.

# Beaver Log Homes/The Sequoyah

Some of the Sequoyah's most important features can't be seen. What you don't see is Beaver Log Homes' unique building system, featuring double tongue-and-grooving and end-notching for a tight fit, with butyl-rubber stripping and saddle gaskets to check air infiltration.

No spiking is necessary with Beaver Log Homes' building system. Close-tolerance saddle-notching, combined with *double* tongue and grooving, holds the uniformly sized logs in place and speeds up log-wall construction.

Various pine species are used in Beaver Log homes and the customer can choose a fully lathed log (no bark) or a "rustic" log, which will be approximately 15 percent bark-covered. Only the pre-cut and labeled wall logs, plus butyl-rubber stripping and saddle gaskets to increase the tightness of construction, are supplied by Beaver Log Homes. Materials like doors, windows, beams, trusses, etc., must be purchased from local sources.

The company does, however, have an interesting variety of construction plans, for homes ranging from 512 to 2,980 square feet in floor area. Beaver Log Homes can also supply custom blueprints based on a sketch, floor plan, or other materials provided by the customer. It's possible to obtain complete and detailed preliminary plans, including floor plans and elevations, before actually placing a purchase order for a log package.

The Sequoyah, one of Beaver Log Homes' 26 stock models, is particularly interesting in that the main body of the house is square and can be ordered in four different sizes: 36 × 36, 40 × 40, 44 × 44, and 48 × 48 feet. As shown in the floor plan, the Sequoyah "40" accommodates three bedrooms and a separate dining room, as well as a breakfast/utility room that connects the main body of the house to the 22 × 22-foot garage.

Log package prices for the Sequoyah range from $7,272 for the Sequoyah "36" to $12,828 for the Sequoyah "48," F.O.B. Claremore, Oklahoma. Beaver Log Homes has dealers in most of the Midwestern and Southwestern states. Some of the dealers are also builders and are available for the erection of Beaver Log homes, if the customer can't or doesn't wish to build the house himself.

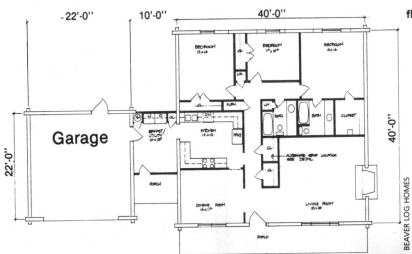

floor plan of the Sequoyah "40"

Wall coverings are unnecessary in a Beaver log home. However, you can use paneling, sheetrock, or wallpaper to create even more unusual and appealing effects.

**The Beaver Log** is a perfectly round, smooth-finished, double tongued-and-grooved, saddle-notched log. It speeds log-wall construction considerably.

the Sequoyah "40," front elevation

45

The dome very possibly is the shape of things to come in a world that has no choice but to become more energy-efficient. And that's not all bad when there are packaged structures as striking as this 35-footer by Cathedralite Domes that can be built for a lot less than the cost of the typical tract house today. With over 800 square feet on the first floor and an easy 300 square feet or more upstairs, it lends itself to a two- or three-bedroom plan.

Domes can be combined with other architectural forms to meet the owner's needs. In this design, the dome has been constructed atop a concrete-block structure that is built into a slope and combines basement, garage, and the entry to the home. The exterior of the dome is finished with a roofing compound that does not require shingling.

With the great variety of door, window, and exterior finishing options, your dome can be as individual as you are. You could have an enormous window of tinted plexiglass, replacing five triangular panels, as here, or a number of skylights fitted into a carefully considered scattering of triangles or half-triangles to lower lighting costs and let you view the stars at night.

An above-ground lower level of conventional straight-wall construction can give you three floors of living space—or two, with a built-in garage and utility room/workshop.

# DOME HOMES

Shelters built more or less in the shape of a dome were among man's earliest constructions, but it wasn't until about 30 years ago that the mathematically precise geodesic dome was developed as a practical working concept and patented by R. Buckminster Fuller. The mathematics of the self-reinforcing, free-span design are so simple, its advantages as a shelter so obvious, that the wonder of it is that Pythagoras, Euclid, or Archimedes didn't set down the formula when making their contributions to the principles of mathematics over 2,000 years ago.

Epitomizing Fuller's dymaxion theory of "doing more with less," the geodesic dome can provide a maximum amount of enclosed space while using a minimum amount of surface materials. From the first doodle in 1927, the brilliantly innovative Fuller envisioned his dome as the mass-produced home of the future. Its first measure of public attention, however, came post-World War II, as a network of austere shelters for the arctic DEW line of early warning radar installations.

Not until the late 1960s, when Fuller became one of the heroes to the counterculture, and domes started popping up in communes from Maine to California, did the general public become conscious of the dome as a home. Constructed largely from "the trash of a wasteful society," the domes of Drop City, in southeastern Colorado, were particularly colorful and funky. Early domers were considered to be freaks, but they showed the way. Even when built with code-conforming, factory-produced materials, domes went up quickly and proved easy to maintain. From approximately 3,000 dome homes built by 1966, there are more than 14,000 scattered across the country today. For many reasons, including the recent proliferation of pre-engineered dome kits, the dome is winning acceptance as a primary, year-round home. Very possibly it is the shape of things to come in a world that has no choice but to become more energy-efficient.

The geodesic dome combines the rigidity of the triangle with the compression strength of the sphere. The structure's entire weight rests on the circular edge, eliminating the need for expensive support walls. Pressure applied at any point, whether from hurricane-force winds or Arctic snow loads, is distributed equally throughout the dome. It is adaptable to all climates, being easy to heat and cool, can fit into most any landscape, and represents substantial savings in construction costs. Not every dome is a geodesic, but most of what follows, other than the specifics on shell assembly, applies to all dome designs.

Dome homes are most easily described as truncated spheres, with the most popular truncations being 3/8, 1/2, and 5/8. This represents the fraction of the sphere employed in the design. The choice of truncation would depend on the interior height desired in relation to floor area. Adequate height is needed if a second floor or sleeping loft is to be included. A 30-foot-diameter 3/8 dome, for instance, offers a maximum height of 12 feet. A 5/8 dome of the same diameter yields a center height of almost 19 feet. Without the benefit of riser walls, an upper level couldn't very well be included in the 3/8 dome.

**The space-frame system is one of the two types of geodesic dome construction. Prefabricated and pre-drilled triangular space frames are simply bolted together to form the shell. Here, the shell is being erected atop a concrete-block riser wall to increase upper-level headroom.**

Riser walls of standard framing lumber are offered as a packaged option by most dome manufacturers. They attach to the foundation and raise the dome a given height (3 feet, for example) to extend second-floor headroom and living space. With smaller domes, the use of risers is sometimes prescribed to facilitate door installation and to accommodate rectangular ventilation windows. Riser walls can also be built from concrete blocks.

As with any kit construction, the foundation is the owner's responsibility and should be prepared in advance of delivery of the materials for the dome. For a dome, the choice of foundation would depend on the contour of the land, the climate, and local building codes. On a hillside, piers and a platform would likely work best. On relatively level ground, concrete slab-on-grade or a wood-floor system set on a continuous-wall concrete foundation with a crawl space or full basement are some of the alternatives.

Basically, there are two types of geodesic assembly, both of which dramatically reduce the number of hours spent on shell construction. One is the hub-and-strut system. The other is the space-frame system. With the hub-and-strut system, modified 2 × 4 or larger struts are linked together with metal connectors or hubs to form the skeletal framework of the dome. After which, pre-cut plywood or composition triangles (the sheathing) are glued and nailed to the framing members. The space-frame system eliminates the need for hubs. Here, factory-assembled triangular space frames, pre-drilled for bolt and wiring holes, are simply bolted together at each angle to form the shell.

With either system, no particular skills or special tools are required to erect the shell. The framework of most dome homes can be put together in a single day, which represents a real labor savings over conventional stud-wall construction. There's little tolerance for error with a dome, but then most systems are color-coded and it's almost impossible to go wrong. Care should be taken, though, to fill all seams with a resilient sealant and then tape them with fiberglass.

Basic dome packages as a rule include no more than the materials needed to complete the multifaceted wood-framed building system. Options include everything from skylights and dormers to sliding-glass doors and perimeter extensions. Placed where you want them, skylights, whether triangular, pentagonal, or hexagonal, will lower lighting costs and let you view the stars at night while you lie in bed. They come tinted to reduce summer heat infiltration, and, properly positioned, they can make an important contribution to passive solar heat gain during the colder months.

The walls are assembled to leave openings at up to five points around the perimeter. The openings allow for the installation of doors, picture windows, dome-to-dome connectors, and straight-wall sections. They also can accommodate rectangular extensions, which, with an outer window wall, sliding-glass door, or solid wall, are like a bay, adding not only floor space, but architectural distinction to the dome. Keep in mind, though, that 4-foot-deep extensions and excessive riser walls can nullify dome-building's lower construction costs and the inherent efficiency of the dome.

All openings in the dome must be framed and sealed to avoid leakage. Those hand-crafted domes of the '60s often had serious leakage problems. But if the joints between adjoining struts and space frames are sealed and conventional roofing is added, there should be no problem.

The hub-and-strut system of geodesic assembly links modified 2 x 4's together with metal connectors to form the framework of the dome. The system shown here also includes framing for the vertical lower level. Other dome manufacturers accomplish the same thing with riser walls of conventional stud-wall construction, though not usually to this height.

There's really no limit to what can be done with a dome architecturally, as this home combining three different shapes proves. The roof treatment of the dome is also unique.

A wide variety of roofing materials can be applied over the plywood skin. Composition shingles are a good choice. They come in many interesting shapes and rich, earthy colors. Hand-split cedar shakes are handsome but tend to be expensive. Fiberglassing is a possibility but takes skill and patience to make it look right. There also are synthetic roofing compounds, such as Neoprene and Hypalon, which, while they don't do much for a dome aesthetically, can be brushed, rolled, or sprayed on. Because the roof is the siding, there is virtually no siding maintenance with a dome.

Some kit manfacturers offer doors, shingles, and other finishing materials, but it may be more economical to purchase such items from local suppliers. Keep the basic package tight and light and it can be shipped inexpensively by motor freight or rail—even coast to coast. Where the factory is within driving distance, you may find it practical to drive to the factory in a van or other small truck and pick up the components yourself. Most manufacturers will also arrange one-way truck rentals for you.

Dome shell prices can be disarmingly low, since the shell often represents less than 25 percent of the *finished* cost of the home. Dome shell prices are far lower proportionally than for most non-dome structures. Also deceptive, a dome *looks* smaller than it is from the outside. Inside, with no load-bearing walls, it can be as big as a barn. The design possibilities are infinite. Offsetting some of the time saved on the shell, more time is required to finish dome interiors.

With all those angles and framing members, insulating the dome can be a real challenge. Some manufacturers recommend the installation of rigid polyurethane-foam insulation on the *outside*, before the roofing is applied. (The R value of two inches of compacted polyurethane is the same as 5 1/2 inches of spun-glass insulation.) With other systems, foamed-in-place insulation could be the easiest way to fill all those recesses on the inside.

Wiring and plumbing are installed in the walls and floor as in any conventional construction. For the interior finish, drywall or sheetrock seem to be the most practical materials. But there's no reason why these walls can't be plastered or paneled. At least one manufacturer offers pre-cut tongue-and-groove pine boards which are fitted together to fill each triangle.

Partitioning is recommended. With open floor plans, the acoustics in a dome can be quite lively. Post-and-beam construction is most often used for the second floor or loft.

A well-constructed dome is virtually airtight, and, with one-third less surface area than conventional construction with the same floor area, heating and cooling expenses are from 35 to 50 percent lower. Dead-air pockets and cold corners are virtually eliminated, permitting the efficient recirculation of heated or cooled air. With the natural flow of air in a dome, the temperature at the floor and vaulted ceiling are nearly equal.

**It's easy to connect two or more domes, and clustering seems likely to become a big factor in dome construction. Here, the connector also provides the angle and roof expanse for an array of solar collectors.**

To heat and cool a dome home, the capacity of the equipment can be scaled down from that needed for conventional, same-size housing. Efficient wood-burning furnaces and stoves should be considered if you build in an area where firewood is plentiful. Other heating-system recommendations would include forced-air, baseboard systems, and radiant heat in the slab. The dome also adapts readily to solar collectors, and several manufacturers offer solar packages as options.

Popular dome sizes are 30, 35, 39, and 45 feet. A spacious three-bedroom dome home can cost as little as $25,000 complete with plumbing and appliances, but not including land. A couple ought to be able to complete a 35-foot dome (1,200-plus square feet) for about $20,000 if they do all their own work. Built by a contractor, it could cost $12,000 to $15,000 more. With the same fixtures inside, getting the same square footage, construction costs average about 15 to 25 percent less than for conventional construction.

Where time or money is a problem, you could build a rather large dome at the outset and add a second floor later. It's also easy to connect two or more domes. A 25- or 26-foot-diameter dome is an ideal size for clustering, which seems likely to become a big factor in residential dome construction. With two or three adjoining structures, rather than a single large dome, you have privacy, sound insulation, and easier temperature regulation. One dome could be used for sleeping, another for daytime activities. The initial dome could be built quickly and economically for use as an immediate residence, with subsequent dome/rooms added when time and budget allow.

# Monterey Domes/Alpine 35

Vertical first-floor walls give the Alpine 35 a high profile for more interior space and headroom on the upper level. The frame uses only one-seventh the structural material needed in a house of similar size, and yet, with the geodesic design, is far stronger.

Monterey Domes utilizes a color-coded hub-and-strut system that makes assembly of its domes simple and mistake-proof. With only a hammer, a wrench, and a stepladder, one man can put up the shell of a Monterey Dome by himself. Unlike prefabricated-space-frame systems, a lot of muscle is not needed during the erection stages. The heaviest piece in the basic Monterey Dome package weighs less than 30 pounds.

Offering 12 different models in two distinctive design series, and diameters from 20 to 45 feet, Monterey Domes has the most complete dome line in the industry. Monterey's Horizon series homes have a low profile—hence, the name. Each dome of the Horizon series has 60 roof triangles and five perimeter openings designed to accept standard doors and windows. There are six different models in this series, with floor areas ranging from 300 to 2,500 square feet.

The Alpine series homes have a high profile and vertical first-floor walls. Additionally, there is more interior space and headroom on the upper floors. Each of the six models in the Alpine series has 90 roof triangles and five perimeter openings. Floor areas range from 400 to 3,500 square feet, with up to two and one half floors.

Monterey Domes' basic package includes all the materials needed to complete the geodesic structural shell: steel hubs; kiln-dried Douglas fir 2 × 4 framing members and studs; triangular plywood panels; bolts, nuts, and washers; nails; construction blueprints; and assembly manual. All parts are pre-cut, color-coded, and ready for assembly.

Once the base triangles have been installed, the framework assembly of a Monterey dome is merely a matter of matching pre-drilled struts and hub flanges of the same color and bolting them together. With most hub-and-strut systems, once the skeletal framework is up, the plywood panels are simply nailed to the struts. But the Monterey system differs here. Pre-cut crossbars and studs, all color-coded, are fitted into each triangle and toe-nailed into place to give superior support for exterior and interior paneling.

After skylight and dormer window positions have been chosen, the triangular panels are installed. With the Monterey Domes system, the panels come in at least two pieces: a base and a cap. Some of the base pieces are further divided into identical half-sections for easier handling.

The basic dome package for the Alpine 35, the model featured here, costs $7,195, F.O.B. Riverside, California. With the compactness of the system, all shipments go at the lowest rate for this type of goods. Approximate shipping cost for a basic Alpine 35 package from Riverside to East Coast destinations would be less than $500.

Among the options for the Alpine 35 are 2-, 3-, 4-, and 5-foot riser-wall packages, priced from $895 to $1,345. Skylights are available in a number of different sizes, shapes, finishes, and lens tints. Opening and fixed models along with optional double glazing are offered. Operable models come with a hand crank and insect screening.

Monterey Domes offers 2 × 6 framing for those areas of the country requiring greater than normal insulation. This option adds 15 percent to the standard price of the basic dome package. Rigid polyurethane-foam insulation is offered, factory-direct, in 2-inch-thick, 4 × 8-foot sheets for a minimum insulation value of R-19. Enough insulation to blanket the Alpine 35 would cost $1,178.

Opening extensions for the Alpine 35 come packaged with pre-cut wood pieces, hardware, and instructions, cost $485, and add 78 square feet of first-floor space.

Solar-energy collectors and storage systems for Monterey Domes are offered through Solar Marketing in Omaha, Nebraska. Each collector system is designed for the Monterey Domes model and the area of the country in which it will be erected.

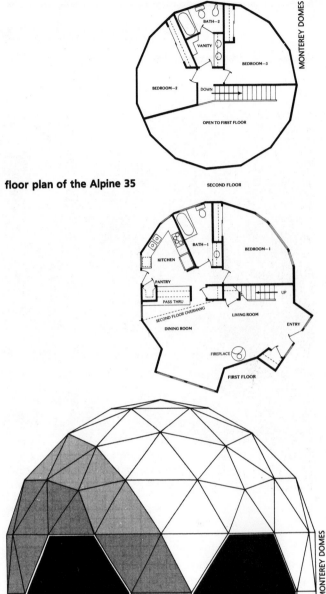

floor plan of the Alpine 35

Alpine 35 profile

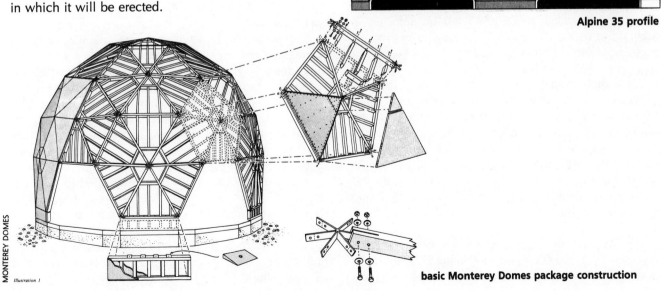

basic Monterey Domes package construction

# Cathedralite Domes/Odyssey 45

If you want a large home at a comparatively inexpensive price, the 45-foot Odyssey dome by Cathedralite could fill your every need. The building begins with 1,500 square feet of first-floor space. It can easily be advanced to 2,300 square feet or more by utilizing the second floor. You can do this while maintaining a huge open ceiling with strategically located skylights.

Cathedralite Domes, with over 2,500 dome homes sold in the past three years, is the world's leading manufacturer of dome structures. The Aptos, California, company offers kits for the construction of dome-home shells in five sizes, ranging from 26 to 45 feet in diameter. In addition to its kits, Cathedralite, through a network of builder/dealers scattered across the U.S., offers complete construction as well as custom services.

The dome home shown is Cathedralite's 45-foot Odyssey, a spectacular, roomy house with from 1,500 to 2,300 square feet of living space, depending on the floor plan used. It is a 3/8 sphere, with five openings, rises 19 feet high, and is assembled by joining 60 prefabricated, triangular space frames. Providing four bedrooms, two full baths, a large living room, dining area, and kitchen, the completed cost can be as low as $25,000 for an owner-built house, or $45,000 if built by a contractor.

The kit price of $8,295, F.O.B. Medford, Oregon, represents only the cost of the shell of the Odyssey 45. In addition to this, a foundation, deck, roofing materials, skylights, doors, insulation, interior finish, plumbing, heating, and wiring are needed to make the dome a home. Also available for this dome are 2-, 3-, and 4-foot riser-wall packages at $1,195, $1,395, and $1,595, respectively.

Cathedralite's space frames are manufactured by bonding precisely milled-and-edged 2 × 4 (or 2 × 6) kiln-dried select Douglas fir spars to a precision-cut triangle (the exterior "skin") of half-inch structural plywood. Nails, staples, and marine resourcinol glue are used to make a space frame that cannot come apart. Holes are pre-drilled in the spars at the factory to ensure perfect alignment when interfacing triangles are snugged together to form the dome.

No crane, hoist, or gin pole is required to raise the dome. The wooden space frames are simply bolted together starting at base plates that have been angle-cut to receive the first frames. A crew of four or five huskies (the average Cathedralite space frame weighs around 75 pounds) shouldn't take more than eight hours to erect a Cathedralite shell.

Shipping weight for the Odyssey 45 package with 2 × 4 framing is 6,400 pounds. With 2 × 6 spars, the package price is $9,695, and the shipping weight is 7,360 pounds. The compactness of the package allows for easy shipment to building sites anywhere in the world.

With domes in five sizes and such options as riser walls, extensions, pentagon- and hexagon-shaped skylights, and canopies, Cathedralite can meet most any customer requirement. The company also offers 30- and 35-foot Vista Domes, which set the dome atop a conventional first-story, pre-framed system.

Nine out of 10 Cathedralite domes are built for use as primary residences, and most buyers design their own floor plan and openings to complement the site. There are no support walls to restrict their ideas. The interior can be finished any way the buyer chooses, but basically the options are the same as with conventional stud-wall construction: sheetrock, plaster, wallpaper, paneling, etc. For an esthetically pleasing and maintenance-free exterior, Cathedralite recommends such proven roof coverings as red cedar shingles or shakes, redwood shakes, asphalt composition shingles, or Neoprene/Hypalon combinations.

For a minimal fee, plus travel expenses, a Cathedralite representative will visit your building site and make recommendations for dome size, type of foundation, and dome placement. If you purchase a dome, the fee is refundable. If you wish to purchase a set of plans to review prior to purchase of a dome, they are available from Cathedralite at $65 for one set or four for $250.

**floor plan of the Odyssey 45**

**The dome kit is strictly the shell of the building. It's up to you or your contractor to customize the interior and exterior to your own specifications. If bedrooms are what you want, this structure could have as many as six, plus your normal living areas. Don't underestimate the volume this building encloses.**

**Using portable scaffolding, and poles to prop up the space frame temporarily, a crew of five shouldn't need more than a day to erect a Cathedralite dome shell. To reach the same point in conventional construction, you would need up to two weeks and considerably more lumber to attain a structurally inferior product.**

# The Big Outdoors People/10-Meter Domes

Designed and built as a lake cabin, this 10-meter dome could also serve as a year-round home. A 39-inch riser wall allows installation of a standard door and basement swing-out or awning-type windows.

The Big Outdoors People's pre-cut, color-coded dome system features a skeletal framework that can be put up in a single day with a single tool—a ratchet wrench. And TBOP supplies the wrench. There are five different domes in TBOP's family of packaged domes, ranging from 26 to 44 feet in diameter—or 7.9 to 13.5 meters. Nevertheless, TBOP regards each plan—and kit—a specific solution to a unique set of problems and works closely with each customer in assessing his needs. The company offers a full range of design services, from on-site planning to custom domes.

TBOP's hub/connector system utilizes wide, high-strength aluminum hubs, with each hub color-coded and drilled to receive up to six struts. Pre-cut to within 1mm tolerance and with end plates attached, the struts, too, are color-coded for their place in the system. End plates are high-strength aluminum wedges with hardened bolts cast in place. The wedges are variously angled to give the dome its shape.

Once all the struts have been connected, completing the skeleton, the skin is installed. The skin is made up of precision-cut triangles of 5/8-inch exterior-grade Blandex (chipboard). The panels, too, are tipped with color to match the strut color code. (You can't go wrong here unless you're color blind.) Glued to the frame with Geotite adhesive, the panels are further secured with coated spiral nails, spaced according to a prescribed pattern.

With the many angles that make up the surface of a dome, the panels, when installed, leave a V-joint where they adjoin. This is filled with a sealant that is compatible to the expansion and contraction of the frame through a 150-degree temperature range—from minus 45 to plus 105 F. The sealant will neither harden nor deteriorate but does require a protective covering. Most of TBOP's dome builders apply H.E.R. (Hydrocide Elastomeric Roofing) or Neoprene and Hypalon. Neoprene is a rubberized base coat. Hypalon is a rubberized color coat used over the Neoprene. These finishing materials can be applied with a roller or spray gun.

Being a Minnesota-based company, most of whose customers build where sub-zero temperatures are the winter norm, TBOP's standard framing strut is the 2 × 6, with up to 2 × 10's available for greater insulation capabilities. The wood is No. 1 grade Douglas fir or southern yellow pine, Dense or SS. These woods have stress ratings over 50 percent stronger than standard construction lumber.

Prices for TBOP's dome-components packages, which include the hub system, 2 × 6 struts, exterior panels, riser wall system, interior dome wall panels (3/8-inch laminated chipboard), and exterior Neoprene/Hypalon coating system, range from $5,010 for a 26-foot dome to $15,685 for a 44-footer. Prices are F.O.B. Wyoming, Minnesota, and do not include entry-door systems, patio sliding doors, or window packages.

For a good line on what a dome costs, the pre-cut kit for TBOP's 10-meter (33-foot), 4/9 sphere, with 800 square feet of living area on the first floor and 200-plus on the second, comes to $10,565, including one insulated entry door and the double-pane window package. From building permits and excavation for the footings and concrete slab to electrical fixtures and the kitchen sink, TBOP estimates the *complete* do-it-yourselfer could bring the dome in for a total of $16,500. Acting as your own contractor and having the work done by professionals would come to $25,775.

Going beyond the dome, TBOP is deeply involved in the development and promotion of alternative life-support systems and includes in its catalog wood-burning stoves, waterless toilets, and solar-heating systems. In addition, TBOP publishes a quarterly newsletter, the *Dome Flyer*. Subscription: $2.50 per year.

**The knocked-down framework for a 10-meter 5/9 dome can be carried in the back of a van with room to spare.**

TBOP's dome home shell comes as a pre-cut, color-coded package of hubs, struts, and precision-cut chipboard triangles and can be easily and quickly erected.

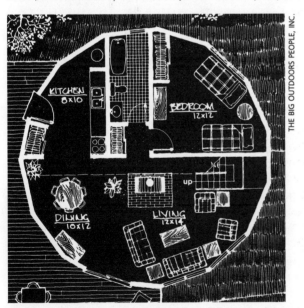

**floor plan of the 10-meter dome**

**The dome's interior wall is ribbed with framing members and under most conditions must be covered. To provide an aesthetic richness in the living or dining room areas, you might consider tongue-and-groove paneling, which has a lot more to offer than the usual chipboard.**

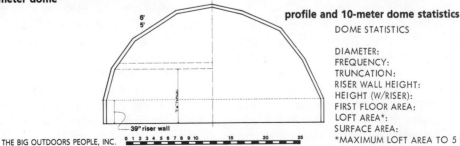

**profile and 10-meter dome statistics**

DOME STATISTICS

| | |
|---|---|
| DIAMETER: | 10 meters (33') |
| FREQUENCY: | 3 |
| TRUNCATION: | 4/9 |
| RISER WALL HEIGHT: | 39 inches |
| HEIGHT (W/RISER): | 16 feet |
| FIRST FLOOR AREA: | 800 sq. ft. gross |
| LOFT AREA*: | 180 sq. ft. |
| SURFACE AREA: | 1650 sq. ft. |

*MAXIMUM LOFT AREA TO 5' HEADROOM LINE

# Geodesic Dome Manufacturing/The Adirondack

One of three models offered in kit form by Geodesic Dome Manufacturing, the 45-foot Adirondack provides up to 2,300 square feet of living area. This does not include the full basement on top of which this particular dome has been built. The dome could also be built on a concrete slab or piers (see page 57). Following the geodesic principle, triangular space frames are bolted together to form a 4 × 4 framework of amazing strength.

Most manufacturers of geodesic dome structures have been in the business only since the early 1970s. But Geodesic Dome Manufacturing Company started out as a dome dealer in 1957 and began manufacturing in 1964. The company holds the first license granted by Buckminster Fuller, having acquired it through purchase from Pease Woodworking Company.

A 3/8 sphere with 1,500 square feet of floor space on the first level, 800 square feet on the second level, the 45-foot-diameter Adirondack is one of three models offered in kit form by Geodesic Dome Manufacturing. The other two are the 26-foot Alpine and the 39-foot Olympic. Like several other Fuller licensees, the building system is based on a prefabricated triangular space frame with exterior-grade plywood glued and stapled to 2 × 4 kiln-dried Douglas fir or western hemlock spars. Interior galvanized metal clips are also applied and perimeter framing members are pre-drilled for bolt assembly, with three bolts to a side.

Once the slab, flooring, or foundation is completed, the dome goes up quickly. With a four- or five-man crew, it can be erected in eight to ten hours. After the first tier of panels is installed, it takes four men to handle the panels—two men holding up the panel, while two more, on scaffolding, bolt it in place.

The next step is placing and sealing the skylights, after which the joints between the space frames are weatherproofed by caulking, followed by Tuff-kote sealant. Fiberglass flashing, 5 1/2 inches wide, is then applied over all exterior joints. Use of the sealants is recommended even if the dome is to be shingled or shaked.

Doors and windows are not included in the basic dome kit, but are offered as options. The additional components and materials needed are readily obtainable from local building-supply dealers. Geodesic Dome Manufacturing ships mostly by common carrier, freight charges collect. If a customer wishes to take advantage of a one-way truck rental, the company will make the arrangements and have the components loaded in a truck for his arrival, ready to be driven back to the job site.

Price for the basic Adirondack kit is $7,790, F.O.B. Plattsburgh, New York. Extras might include up to five (for a 45-foot dome) hexagon- or pentagon-shaped skylights or skydomes at from $390 to $706 each, a 6-foot Andersen gliding door at $535, and wood-framed, insulated-glass wing panels at $450 a pair.

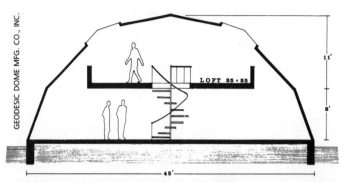

isometric plan, lower level, of the Adirondack

**Since there are no support walls to restrict your ideas, you're free to take maximum advantage of the space inside your dome home—with a vaulted ceiling soaring above you, floating partitions, a balustraded balcony, and windows and skylights placed where you want them.**

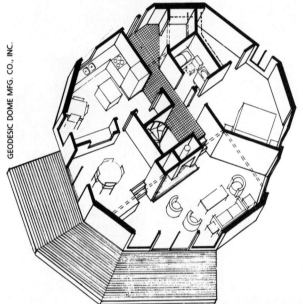

profile of the Adirondack

# Shelter Construction and Development/The Glencairn

The design of the dome is left to the customer when he builds with a Shelter Construction kit. Shelter sells only the basic shell-building components. This 28 1/2-foot-diameter 5/8 dome, built near Mansfield, Ontario, is a passive solar design. Heating, with electricity and wood, costs under $150 per winter.

Operating on the basis that all construction beyond the dome framework is standard construction and can best be done by the owner-builder or contractors utilizing local materials, Shelter Construction and Development Ltd.'s principal stock in trade are hubs and struts, with pre-cut triangular panels an option.

Shelter provides a free design service for its customers and tailors to order basic drawings which a knowledgeable builder should be able to follow for preparing the foundation and installing the ground floor. Detailed directions are given for easy assembly of the dome. Where detailed working drawings are required for bids or for mortgage approvals, Shelter will provide custom working drawings for about $300.

Framing kits include hub connectors, pre-cut 2 × 4 spruce struts, and all nuts, bolts, and washers needed to complete the assembly. The frame only for the 28 1/2-foot Glencairn, a 5/8 dome, costs $1,975 F.O.B. Toronto, Canada, or Lewisberry, Pennsylvania. A complete set of pre-cut 3/8-inch fir panels, ready to be nailed to the skeletal framework, also costs $1,975. However, Shelter will freely provide all panel dimensions, should the owner-builder prefer to cut his own triangles from standard 4 × 8 sheets of plywood.

The three-bedroom Glencairn is 18 feet tall and easily accommodates a second floor. The first floor measures approximately 630 square feet. Where 2 × 4's do not allow for the installation of sufficient insulation, Shelter can provide 2 × 6 or 2 × 8 struts.

The big window on the Mansfield, Ontario, passive solar dome faces south and is double glazed. The floor of the dome is a concrete heat sink and the walls have an insulating value of R-30. Even without a "solar package," most domes are twice as energy-efficient as conventional structures of comparable size.

Putting panels on the framework of a 40-foot dome. With 2 x 4 spruce spars, the framework can be put up for $3,200. Pre-cut triangular plywood panels to cover the erected frame would cost about the same from Shelter Construction. With the dimensions provided, they also could be cut by the owner-builder from standard sheets of 4 x 8 plywood.

**cross-section plan of the Glencairn**

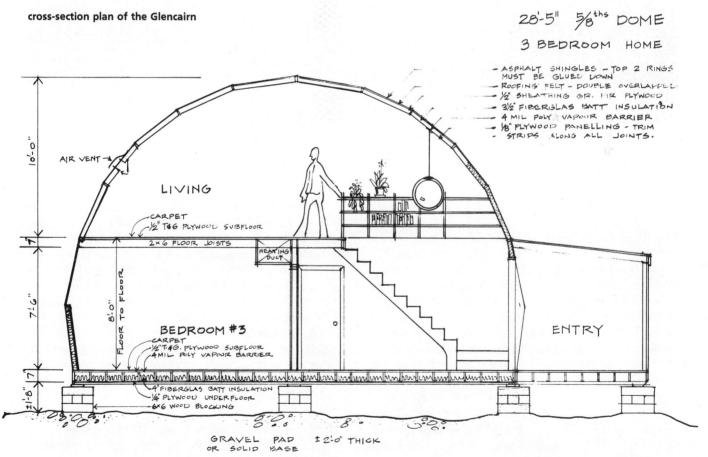

28'-5" ⅝ths DOME
3 BEDROOM HOME

- ASPHALT SHINGLES - TOP 2 RINGS MUST BE GLUED DOWN
- ROOFING FELT - DOUBLE OVERLAPPED
- ½" SHEATHING GR. FIR PLYWOOD
- 3½" FIBERGLAS BATT INSULATION
- 4 MIL POLY VAPOUR BARRIER
- ⅛" PLYWOOD PANELLING - TRIM STRIPS ALONG ALL JOINTS.

SHELTER CONSTRUCTION AND DEVELOPMENT LTD.

# American Geodesic/Omegadome

In mathematical terms, the Omegadome is "a modified 3-frequency, alternate-breakdown, icosahedron-based geodesic dome blended with traditional vertical rectilinear architecture." But all you really need to know is that it produces an attractive, versatile, and economic shelter.

The Omegadome by American Geodesic, Inc., blends the strength and economy of geodesics with traditional rectilinear architecture. Depending on the type of foundation prepared for it, the shell can be erected and weatherproofed in from 60 to 80 man-hours, or in about three days by a three-man crew. The same wide variety of roofing materials, siding, doors, and windows can be used as with conventional wood-frame construction.

Basically, the Omegadome, with 830 square feet of floor space, is a 1/4 dome, as opposed to the usual 3/8, 1/2, or 5/8 truncation. The resultant shell is further intersected to create three vertical walls. These sidewalls and the three kneewalls are all load bearing. Additional strength and stability is gained by using welded steel braces in the dome shell. The 16-inch-high kneewalls are retained by steel rods anchored in the concrete base or deck-support system.

To form the geodesic shell, 39 prefabricated triangular panels, assembled from custom-milled 2 × 6 spars and exterior-grade plywood, are bolted together in sequence. The Omegadome kit also includes nine pre-assembled wall panels. Each wall when installed leaves an opening about 7 feet high and 13 feet wide to receive framing, doors, and windows according to the customer's design.

The Omegadome has been adapted for erection on a wood deck and full-perimeter foundation (System 1); wood deck on posts or pads (System 2); or concrete slab (System 3). Systems 1 and 2 include a Geodeck package, with color-coded and ready-to-assemble 2 × 10 or 2 × 12 stringers and headers and 2 × 8 joists. With base prices of $8,950, $8,350, and $6,350, respectively, F.O.B. Bangor, Maine, for the three kits, the manufacturer estimates the owner-builder can put up an Omegadome on an improved parcel of land for $10,000 to $13,500. These are *minimum* prices but include everything from foundation to plumbing. If built by a contractor, figure an additional $9,000 to $12,000. American Geodesic provides blueprints for concrete work, setting of posts, and construction of a wood deck as needed.

A variety of roofing materials, including asphalt roll roofing, asphalt and fiberglass shingles, machine-cut white cedar shingles, and hand-split red cedar shakes, has been used on Omegadomes. The first is the most economical, the last the most expensive. Vinyl, epoxy, and Neoprene roof coatings also have been applied with success. The roof area of the Omegadome measures approximately 1,200 square feet. Any insulation applicable with wood-frame construction can be used in an Omegadome. The insulation surface is roughly 2,000 square feet for any Omegadome design. Sheetrock, plaster, plywood/plastic paneling, tongue-and-groove pine, etc., can be economically applied to the interior of the geodesic panels and vertical wall sections.

Complete shell packages, including doors, windows, siding, and roofing, are offered for delivery in New England. But for delivery to other states, American Geodesic has found it's to the customer's advantage to obtain from local sources those construction materials that are not peculiar to the Omegadome. This allows for the widest choice of finishing materials and the economy of direct purchase. To save on shipping costs, Omegadome buyers can pick up their packages at the factory, if they choose. An 8 × 20-foot flatbed trailer will accommodate a basic System 3 package.

American Geodesic also offers hub-and-strut-system domes, in seven models, from 30 to 49 feet in diameter.

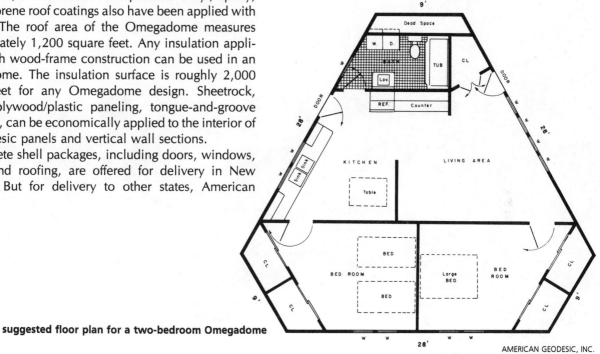

**suggested floor plan for a two-bedroom Omegadome**

The Omegadome can be erected on a concrete slab, as shown here, or on a full foundation or concrete pads or posts. A Geodeck package, consisting of pre-cut and color-coded stringers, headers, and joists is offered as an option for use with the latter systems.

The Omegadome kit consists of 39 ready-to-bolt-together dome panels, plus nine vertical wall panels of custom-cut 2 x 6's and exterior-grade plywood. It can be erected in about three days by a three-man crew.

# Galaxy Homes/The Yaca-Dome

The Yaca-Dome is a dome home with more than a few differences, not the least of which is the fact that it is not a geodesic design.

Galaxy Homes' Yaca-Dome, which gets its name from designer Joseph Yacaboni, has more than 10,000 pounds of structural steel in its roof system and is virtually indestructible. Erected on a 50-foot-diameter concrete slab or outer ring in which 20 anchor bolts have been pre-embedded, the steel framework of the Yaca-Dome can be assembled in about six hours by a three-man crew.

The dome package includes 20 curved steel "T" beams, each 30 feet long and weighing 310 pounds. These are raised into position by a crane or an improvised boom and are then bolted to a central hub and secured at the base. Once the steel is up, the roof panels are installed, using caulking and sealant for complete weatherproofing. There are 20 roof panels and they're the sandwich type, with a tough fiberglass skin and a 3-inch core of rigid urethane-foam insulation. After the shell is erected, the dome ceiling must be sprayed to a half-inch thickness of Zonolite 3300 or the equivalent to meet building-code, fire-safety requirements.

A wide variety of exterior materials, as well as door and window designs, can be used for the 20 vertical wall sections, which are 6 feet wide and non-bearing. To keep costs down, the builder could use 2 × 4-stud-wall construction and an exterior of textured Masonite or plywood. A stucco exterior is another possibility. Galaxy does offer a wall-package option, with panels similar in composition to the roof panels—fiberglass skin and a rigid foam core. Here, the builder would add drywall or paneling for the interior finish after completing his electrical installation. To flood the dome with light and take advantage of the views, sliding-glass doors, all-glass view walls, and round picture windows can be installed.

This distinctive dome home measures 38 feet in diameter, for a floor area of nearly 1,150 square feet. The interior arrangement is limited only by the imagination of the owner. A circular center loft of 200 or more square feet can be added with no major structural changes. A steel loft ring, in two sections, weighing 250 pounds each, and 10 loft support rods are included in the basic Yaca-Dome package, the price of which is $15,500, F.O.B. Escondido, California.

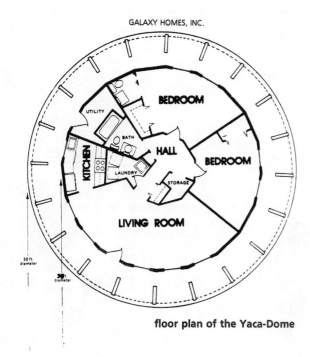

floor plan of the Yaca-Dome

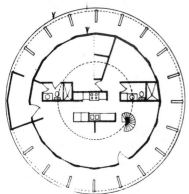

Once the steel has been erected, the insulated fiberglass roof panels are slipped into place and secured to the curved "T" beams with screws, 12 per panel, from the underside.

A circular center loft can be installed with no major structural changes. The steel loft ring and support rods are included in the basic Yaca-Dome kit. The stairs are extra.

# Tension Structures/The O'Dome

The O'Dome may be a little tight for use as a full-time residence, but there's nothing to prevent you from joining two together for more living space.

Unlike most of the dome homes being built today, Tension Structures' O'Dome is designed more for recreational rather than residential use. William Moss, famous designer of the Pop Tent and other outdoor-living products, developed the super ellipsoid 10 years ago as his own summer home. Moss constructed his first O'Dome (or Unidome) from 20 flexed-plywood panels, each a skinny 12-foot-long triangle with a 4-foot base. Today, the design is essentially the same but the material is different.

The all-seasons, flame-retardant, maintenance-free O'Dome, measuring 25 feet in diameter, is assembled from factory-molded panels that bond an insulating slab of compressed urethane and a steel base plate between outer layers of tough fiberglass. The panels are shipped nearly flat and are bent into final position during assembly. The tension created by the bending contributes to the dome's superior strength.

Adjoining panels are locked together for a weather-tight seal by plastic tongue-and-groove extrusion and anchored to the deck by lag bolts or rawl plugs at two points. A metal securing ring holds the tips and frames the skylight opening. Additional tension is provided by a steel aircraft cable threaded horizontally through each panel at the hip and secured at the door frame.

Installation of the doorway (or doorways) and skylight complete the exterior of the structure. Four panels come with pre-engineered window openings.

It shouldn't take more than two days for a crew of three to put up an O'Dome. Erected on a wood or concrete deck, the O'Dome provides 10 feet of headroom at the center and 530 square feet of unobstructed living space for the builder to partition and furnish as he chooses.

The O'Dome can be ordered in a choice of four colors—white, blue, green, or beige; all one color or in combinations. The standard package includes panels; two complete entrance systems, each 8 feet wide and including sliding-glass doors; four two-piece windows; and all necessary hardware. Price of the kit is $6,150, F.O.B. Plymouth, Michigan. Packaged in 16 to 20 boxes, shipping weight is approximately 3,000 pounds. The heaviest box weighs 170 pounds, and the longest dimension is 16 feet 2 inches.

Two or more O'Domes can easily be joined to create more living space. Units also can be disassembled and moved elsewhere. Maintenance? No problem. The exterior surface is smooth-molded gelcoat. Simply hose down the dome occasionally. That's all it takes to keep it looking new.

### floor plan of the O'Dome

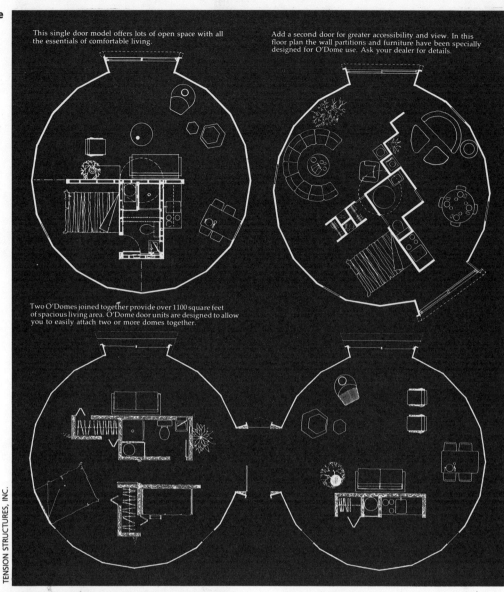

This single door model offers lots of open space with all the essentials of comfortable living.

Add a second door for greater accessibility and view. In this floor plan the wall partitions and furniture have been specially designed for O'Dome use. Ask your dealer for details.

Two O'Domes joined together provide over 1100 square feet of spacious living area. O'Dome door units are designed to allow you to easily attach two or more domes together.

TENSION STRUCTURES, INC.

TENSION STRUCTURES, INC.

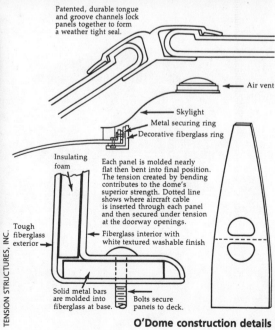

Patented, durable tongue and groove channels lock panels together to form a weather tight seal.

← Air vent
← Skylight
← Metal securing ring
← Decorative fiberglass ring

Insulating foam

Each panel is molded nearly flat then bent into final position. The tension created by bending contributes to the dome's superior strength. Dotted line shows where aircraft cable is inserted through each panel and then secured under tension at the doorway openings.

Tough fiberglass exterior

Fiberglass interior with white textured washable finish

Solid metal bars are molded into fiberglass at base.

Bolts secure panels to deck.

**O'Dome construction details**

65

In its simplest form, the A-frame is one of the easiest of all houses to construct. It can be built on a wooden deck, poles, a concrete slab, or a continuous-masonry-wall foundation.

The 24 x 36-foot Lucerne by Vacation Land Homes provides ample space under its roof to accommodate three bedrooms and a 500-square-foot dining/living area with a distinctive sky-high window wall.

The modified design of the Alpine, one of the Vacation Land Homes' most popular A-frames, adds drama to its appearance and a functional interior layout easily adaptable to many different arrangements.

# A-FRAMES

Designed to shrug off everything from heavy snows to hurricane winds, the distinctive shape of the self-bracing A-frame made this building style the new favorite of vacation-home builders in the 1950s. For a while, it threatened to outnumber the trees. In its simplest form, it's still the easiest of all houses to construct and, for floor area, next to the dome, the least expensive.

We don't know who built the first A-frame, but, as a hard-sided "tent," it seems a natural progression from the simple shelter tents that millions of American males became acquainted with in scouting and in military service during World War II. With the do-it-yourself movement that burgeoned in the post-war years, the A-frame cottage became a possible dream, adaptable to every type of vacationland site.

More than half the orders filled by some of the biggest plans services during that era were for A-frame designs. The materials called for in most plans then cost under $2,000 (for the shell) and aimed toward the use of standard lumber items, with modular design, regular frame spacing, and openings sized for stock windows. And that's pretty much the key to the A-frame's continuing popularity. Simplicity—both in design and construction.

The typical A-frame is built on a wooden deck supported by concrete piers. Using a template to ensure the accuracy of the angle, frames are assembled on the ground before being raised into position. Joists for a loft or second floor, if called for, represent the bar of the "A." Roof/wall sheathing can double as the inside wall and is either tongue-and-groove decking, applied horizontally, or 4 × 8-foot plywood panels nailed directly to the rafters. End walls are largely glass to flood the "tunnel" with sunlight.

Requiring no bearing walls, the A-frame can be adapted to any floor plan and life-style, whether for use as a ski lodge, beach house, mountain cabin, or poolside cabana. It also can be built on a concrete slab, poles, or a continuous masonry-wall foundation. Most designs allow for easy expansion, generally in 2-, 4-, or 6-foot increments, depending on frame spacing.

For all its sturdy practicality, the A-frame is not without drawbacks. For one, there's all that lost space, at the top, and at the sides, near the floor. There's also a tendency to underinsulate, especially when tongue-and-groove sheathing is used. Owners are understandably reluctant to conceal that handsome face and don't always have the foresight to install rigid foam insulation between the sheathing and the shingles. In snow country, you need more than sheathing and shingles to keep out the cold. And at the seashore, without adequate insulation, the upper reaches of an A-frame can reach oven temperatures.

Another snow-country problem is encountered with roof/walls that nearly touch the ground. Tons of snow and ice can bank against the windward side of the structure, creating unequal lateral forces that can shift even a firmly anchored A-frame or cave in the roof. That's why A-frames in winter ski areas, today, often are built atop masonry sidewalls or a first floor of conventional construction—and are more chalet than "A."

There are many possible modifications of the "straight A." The sharply sloping roof does not lend itself to installation of windows in the same plane, but dormers can provide cross ventilation and balance the intense light from the ends. Another modification is to add a wing, or wings, of conventional straight-wall construction. The newest trend is the truncated "A," sometimes called an "engel frame," with a mansard-style roof. With the walls less severely angled and the sharp peak eliminated, almost all of the interior space can be made to work. Heating and cooling also are less of a problem.

Installation of wiring, water lines, and ductwork is no challenge in an A-frame. Simply lay the conduits in the angle formed by floor and wall. And if you're clever, built-ins can straighten up the wall at least to waist level and solve storage problems.

With chalets, domes, and log houses capturing much of the market that would have gone to pre-cut A-frames a decade ago, several kit manufacturers have dropped their A-frame designs. But at least half a dozen companies continue to supply A-frame packages.

# TimberLodge/The Chal-A

TimberLodge's redwood Chal-A can be provided with or without vertical sidewalls for erection on any type of foundation. Designed for the most stringent load conditions, the Chal-A is available in 20- and 24-foot widths, in any length that is multiple of 4 feet.

Built of redwood, one of nature's most perfect building materials, TimberLodge's Chal-A is offered in 20- and 24-foot widths, in any length that is a multiple of four feet. The loft also can be ordered in lengths that are multiples of four.

TimberLodge's basic A-frame measures 20 × 32 feet and features a 240-square-foot loft. Units can be provided with or without vertical sidewalls for erection on any type of foundation. The basic package is for erection on a reinforced slab foundation or reinforced wood sub-floor over a crawl space or basement.

The kit includes pre-cut rafters, loft floor joists, and 2 × 8-inch tongue-and-groove roof decking and loft flooring—all the materials needed to complete the redwood shell, plus stairs with open treads from floor to loft, a redwood door with frame, a sliding-glass door with tempered insulating glass, and all required hardware. Not included are finish flooring, roofing felt, and shingles. Fixed end-wall windows include glazing stops, but no glass.

Price of the basic TimberLodge Chal-A package is $11,196, F.O.B. North Kansas City, Missouri. The components are manufactured in northern California and shipped by rail to Kansas City, where substantial stocks are maintained. TimberLodge claims to be the nation's largest builder and distributor of pre-cut redwood homes. If you're concerned about the use of redwood in construction, TimberLodge cuttings do not exceed replacement growth of this renewable but limited natural resource.

TimerLodge furnishes detailed foundation plans and erection instructions. Installation of the foundation and the sub-floor can proceed during the period required to get the components package to the building site.

Shipping weight for the basic package is approximately 19,500 pounds. Material for a redwood deck is an option at $381 for every 4 × 20-foot increment. A redwood interior partitioning package for the standard plan, including loft and stair railings, costs $1,854. Insulation packages are offered for all climates.

TimberLodge manufactures three general types of homes—A-frame, chalet, and ranch—for do-it-yourself or to save time on turn-key construction. The completed costs of most TimberLodge houses are on a par with conventional construction. What you save here in erection costs, using pre-cut parts, you spend for a better material—redwood.

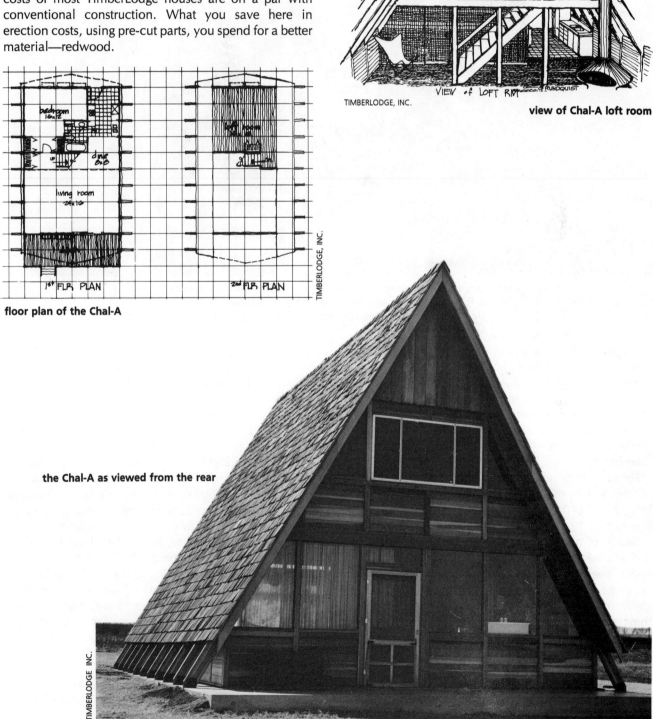

floor plan of the Chal-A

view of Chal-A loft room

the Chal-A as viewed from the rear

# Forest Homes/The Midi Chalet

With short, vertical sidewalls and a good deal of gingerbread, the Midi Chalet is an A-frame putting on airs, but an A-frame, nevertheless. Cedar shakes, decks, dormers, and length extensions are among the options.

It might seem incongruous that a kit manufacturer known for its "desert-style" homes is also a leading producer of A-frames. But that's the case with Forest Homes, which markets mostly in the Southwest. There are four different A-frames in this Arizona manufacturer's line, ranging in size from the 16 × 24-foot Mini Chalet (an A-frame with pretensions) to the 28 × 40-foot Lakeside A.

Forest Homes sells both shell and interior kits for construction by the owner. Any of its houses can also be bought as a dealer-erected shell or as a turn-key structure.

Much of the wall system of a Forest Home is prefabricated, which makes owner-erection that much easier. The standard do-it-yourself kit includes prefabricated wall sections, flooring, 2 × 6-inch tongue-and-groove decking, felt underlayment, insulation, asphalt shingles, partially prefabricated interior bearing walls and loft, siding as required, exterior doors and windows, the stair system, and all necessary nails, bolts, and hardware.

Forest Homes' smaller A-frames—the Mini Chalet and the Midi Chalet (pictured)—have short, vertical sidewalls and come with a good deal of gingerbread. The two larger models—the Brookside A and the Lakeside A—have more traditional A-frame styling, with the roof extending down to the deck. However, if you're hooked on Heidi, a "chalet" front is an option with both the Brookside and the Lakeside. Cedar shakes, dormers, decks, and 8-foot extensions are among the other options.

Prices for Forest Homes' A-frames begin at $6,595, for the Mini Chalet shell kit, F.O.B. Mesa, Arizona. An interior kit, with sheetrock, electrical system, plumbing and fixtures, kitchen cabinets and countertops, range and oven, interior doors, etc., is an option at $4,100. For the 988-square-foot Midi Chalet, these prices are $9,695 and $4,700, respectively. For a good line on what you might save by doing it yourself, Forest Homes' price for a turn-key Midi Chalet, built on your lot by a Forest Homes contractor, would be approximately $30,000 (septic tank not included). Shell kit prices for the 1,287-square-foot Brookside A and the 1,526-square-foot Lakeside A are $11,195 and $12,995, respectively.

Forest Homes' other models include ranch-style houses, an interesting selection of hexagons, and seven models in its Desert Series.

Forest Homes' larger A-frames, the Brookside and the Lakeside, have more traditional A-frame styling, with the roof extending down to the deck. If you like gingerbread, a "chalet" front is an option with both models.

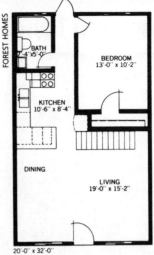

floor plan of the Midi Chalet

## The Lakeside A-Frame
BY FOREST HOMES

## The Brookside A-Frame
FOREST HOMES / BY FOREST HOMES

71

# Vacation Land Homes/The Mansard

The truncated A-frame with a mansard-type roof and modified wall cant is a more functional design, providing maximum living space and no heat wasted from high, peaked gables.

Vacation Land Homes has been one of the country's most successful builders of lakeside and hunting-lodge-type homes for more than two decades. From its versatile series of designs, a functional leisure-time home can be pre-cut to fit any family's requirements and to fit into virtually any setting.

The company offers 25 homes in 39 plans and will customize any of these to satisfy a customer's needs and preferences. The bulk of this manufacturer's business has been in low-cost, two-bedroom cottages. But there also are three-story, five-bedroom chalets, and contemporary, stacked-module designs (see page 133) for year-round suburban or country living.

Included in the Vacation Land line are several A-frames. The popular 20 × 32-foot Clearwater and the 24 × 36-foot Lucerne are straight-A designs, with roof/walls rising to the familiar apex. The very roomy Alpine is a modified straight-A with wings on both sides. It's the contemporary styling of the Mansard, however, that best exemplifies Vacation Land's experience and creativity. This more-functional, truncated A-frame has three bedrooms on two levels and no heat loss from high, peaked gables. With the modified wall cant, there's no wasted space, either.

The basic Mansard, shown here, measures 24 × 36 feet, not including 8 × 24-foot decks at front and rear. Both decks and the second-floor porch receive protection from roof overhangs. Inside, the two-level window wall, second-floor balcony, and open-beam cathedral ceiling in the living/dining area contribute much to the feeling of spaciousness.

One modification of this model provides for a large sun deck on the flat roof. It's reached by a decorative spiral staircase from the second-floor porch. Railing options include chain-on-beam, wrought iron, or chalet spindles. There's also a 24 × 40-foot version of the Mansard, with space for an additional bathroom on the second floor.

Price for the basic Mansard package, which includes everything for the shell except the wood floor, is $23,582, F.O.B. Bellaire, Michigan. For double-wall construction, the price is $25,015. A large network of Vacation Land dealers is equipped to supply not only building services, but any necessary "extras." This would include those hand-split cedar shingles, which are an option.

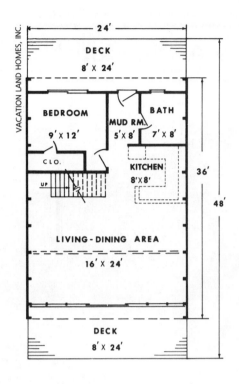
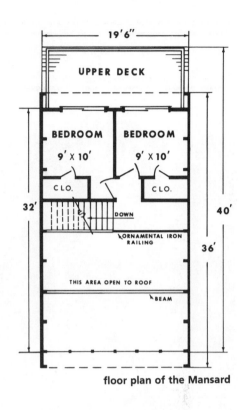

floor plan of the Mansard

73

# Easy A/The Mod A

Erection is quick, maintenance is nil, with Easy A's pre-engineered steel structures. They not only prove there's more than one way to build an A-frame at a reasonable cost, but come in a choice of colors. At left is the Mod A; at right is the Maxi-Mod.

The pre-engineered A-frames offered in kit form by the Easy A Division of Southern Structures are steel constructions, designed to withstand not only heavy snow loads, but hurricane-force winds. Assembly is quick and easy. The framing is bolted together from sections of Struct-A-Frame and (for the loft) Struct-A-Joist. Everything is pre-cut, punched, drilled, and coded for position. As with other A-frames, these easygoing structures are completely self-supporting. No load-bearing walls are needed.

Easy A's A-frames come in four models: the Classic A; the Mod A; the Maxi-Mod A; and the Mini-Mod A. The last three are truncated versions of the Classic A. The Easy A's can be erected on a concrete slab, continuous-masonry-wall foundation, or pilings. With anything but a slab, however, it's necessary to install a sub-floor system. The building frames are spaced at 6-foot intervals and must be firmly secured to steel anchor plates embedded in reinforced concrete.

End walls, assembled from pre-cut tongue-and-groove planking, V-grooved inside and out, can be ordered with a choice of doors and windows. A pre-engineered flooring system for above-grade construction, dormer sidewall windows, a spiral staircase, and finishing items are available. Southern Structures even offers a compact kitchen/bath module that includes all plumbing fixtures, a pre-wired electrical panel to provide 200-ampere service, a 30-gallon quick-recovery water heater, and a furnace for central heating. Air conditioning can be added to the module.

The roof/walls of the Easy A's are built up with insulated polyboard before the ribbed weatherspan—architectural panels of Korad-laminated, 26-gauge galvanized steel—is installed. There are six color options for the maintenance-free roof/wall panels: blue, off-white, green, burnt orange, tan, and brown.

The Mod A, shown here in the sun-deck version, and the Classic A and the Maxi, all come in 24-foot widths, with lengths beginning at 24 feet. The units can be lengthened in increments of 6 feet. The basic Mini-Mod measures 17 × 18 feet. It, too, can be stretched. Kit price for the basic 24 × 24-foot Mod A is $8,470, F.O.B. Lafayette, Louisiana. With sun deck, the price is $9,198. For every 6 feet of extension, add $1,064. The basic kits do not include flooring materials.

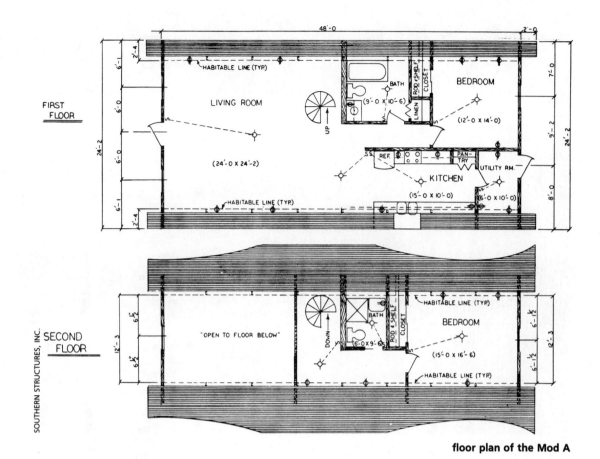

floor plan of the Mod A

The framing of the Mod A is sheathed with insulated polyboard before the maintenance-free, ribbed weatherspan is installed.

The low-profile Maxi-Mod is designed to fill many needs, from a garage to a family dwelling. The building size begins at 24 x 24 feet and the length can be increased in 6-foot increments.

The soaring roof line decked with picturesque trim gives American Timber Homes' chalet the flavor of Switzerland and the lofty Alps. The walk-out basement, creating three levels of living space, is one of the many builder options with this aristocrat of A-frame-type homes.

Many of the log manufacturers include chalet designs in their portfolios. Whether nestled in the Colorado wilderness or overlooking the Blue Ridge Mountains or sitting at the edge of a clear New England lake, Real Log Homes' Aspen is a home for all regions.

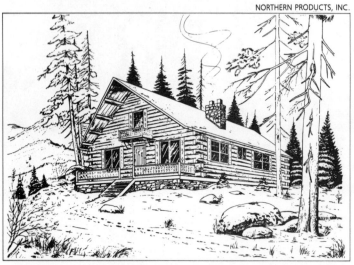

Northern Products' Kennebec is another handsome log home with the flair of a Swiss chalet. The bold log walls and distinctive roof line blend quietly with any surroundings.

# CHALETS

A Swiss chalet can be anything from a herdsman's hut in the Alps to a posh St. Moritz ski lodge with a dozen guest rooms. There also are Austrian, Bavarian, French, and Italian versions of the chalet. So we don't draw any fine lines when it comes to defining the domestic variety. For the purpose of this book, a chalet is a one-and-one-half to three-story house with a gable roof, large front windows, open porches, extended eaves, and, often, extensive decorative woodwork on the exterior. It may or may not have a yodeling balcony.

Chalets generally are large houses with a finished loft and an open-beamed cathedral ceiling over a living room that wouldn't ring true without a large fireplace and a front-facing window wall to the great outdoors. A chalet is at its best wherever there's a great view—whether that's ski country, lakeside, or beachfront. Out of the mountains, though, chalets tend to look out of place, especially if covered with gingerbread. They are particularly suited to wooded lots and are built mostly for use as ski lodges. Just looking at a chalet should suggest snowy mountaintops.

Some pre-cut chalets are little more than elevated A-frames, built atop a walk-out basement. A full basement, though, creating a third level of living space, is common with chalets. When you've got to go that deep to get below the frost line for your footings, you might as well include a basement. As a rule, it's the most economical floor space obtainable. If you build on a slope, you can easily incorporate a daylight lower level.

The design of a chalet, with its Old World flavor, often is more complicated than that of other pre-cut structures intended primarily for recreation use. As a multi-level structure with decks that sometimes are cantilevered, and balconies and extended eaves, it is not an easy project for the inexperienced builder. A chalet also can be a good deal more expensive to build, especially when structural and other modifications are required for areas with extra-heavy snowfalls.

You won't find much stud-wall construction in chalet designs. Most of it is post-and-beam or single-log wall. Indeed, many of the log manufacturers offer chalet-styled log houses, and, as chalets go, these are among the easiest to build.

For year-round residential use, extensions are sometimes added to basic chalet designs, utilizing the chalet for family living and the extension for a separate, quiet bedroom wing.

**As with this Pacific Frontier Homes chalet, the living area of the chalet almost always is left open to a beamed cathedral ceiling. Sidewalls, unlike a regular A-frame, are at least head-high.**

# Lindal Cedar Homes/The Marvista

The Marvista could safely be called a contemporary chalet. Offering a sweeping, two-story view, it's from Lindal's recently introduced Prow Series, which has become one of the company's best sellers. A prow front can also be added to any of Lindal's other chalet designs.

Lindal Cedar Homes, with over 150 independent distributors throughout North America, is one of the most widely known of the pre-cut home manufacturers. No matter where you plan to build—and Lindal homes have been shipped to virtually every corner of the globe—a Lindal pre-cut package can bring it all home.

Lindal used to be known for its budget pre-cuts. But the company no longer offers A-frames and smaller versions of its Beach series. The newest designs are for sizable, quality structures, both traditional and contemporary in style. Only three of the current designs are for houses of under 1,000 square feet.

Lindal offers 16 design series, with 48 plans, ranging from the two-bedroom, 726-square-foot Bikini beach house in the View series, to the 2,789-square-foot Lincoln in the Presidential series. Its new Prow series has become an instant hit and is represented here by the spectacular Marvista.

Like all Lindal houses, the 1,835-square-foot Marvista is built from kiln-dried western red cedar, a wood with natural warmth and enduring appeal. It ages beautifully and demands little care. The basic Prow has a sweeping two-story, two-sided view through a vast panorama of glass. The smallest unit in this series is the 1,250-square-foot Vista, which is the Marvista without wings. Largest is the 2,020-square-foot Buena Vista. The deck, which is optional, can be designed to wrap around any of these units to match the prow configuration and heighten the drama. Inside, there's the natural drama of wood-planked cathedral ceilings and exposed beams.

Construction is post-and-beam, with 4 × 4 or larger fir columns supporting the roof system. Roof and loft beams are 4 × 10 Steelam, consisting of bands of sawtooth-edged steel sandwiched between two 2 × 10 fir or hemfir timbers—all pre-stressed and pre-cambered under 500,000 pounds of pressure. Gables are pre-cut and shipped in panelized sections, ready to install. Wall planks (applied vertically), floor, and roof decking are all tongue-and-grooved for easier assembly.

Lindal pre-cuts are sold in Basic, Plus, and Custom packages. The Basic package does not include roof and wall insulation, interior wall and roof liner, inside doors or floor underlayment. The Plus package includes particle-board floor underlayment, 3 inches of roof and wall insulation, tight-knot-pine wall and roof liner, spaced rather than solid roof sheathing, inside doors, and cedar shingles (instead of the Basic's asphalt shingles). The Custom package upgrades the interior wall and roof liner from pine to tight-knot cedar and the roofing to cedar shakes. Prices for the pre-cut Marvista kit are $33,263, $41,389, and $46,979, respectively, F.O.B. Tacoma, Washington.

Although assembly time may be affected by many variables, it's entirely feasible to erect a Lindal to shell stage in less than three weeks. An experienced three-man crew could probably put up the Marvista in 12 days.

Other Lindal chalets include the more traditional Norway, Grenoble, Banff, and Whistler in the Chalet series. Measuring from 1,018 to 1,987 square feet, all of these designs feature a living room with cathedral ceiling, open beams, and a window wall. A loft extends the living area upstairs. Lindal's Chalet Star series, with three designs, measuring from 2,006 to 2,235 square feet, utilizes the chalet for family living and adds an extension for a separate, quiet bedroom wing.

Any Lindal plan can be modified. You can move doors, windows, even walls. You can even arrange to build a Lindal based on your own original design.

**Lindal's patented Steelam roof and loft beams consist of a solid band of sawtooth-edged steel encased between two 2 x 10 fir or hemfir timbers—all pre-stressed and pre-cambered under 500,000 pounds of pressure.**

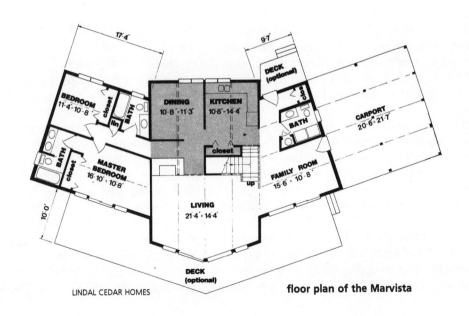

floor plan of the Marvista

# Justus/The Timberline

With the Timberline's unique bay window, the view of the outside world is virtually unobstructed. The Timberline can be modified to meet extreme conditions and is ideal for snow country.

Justus Company manufactures pre-cut solid cedar homes. The houses are built of 4 × 8-inch kiln-dried western red cedar wall timbers and utilize approximately three times the quantity of wood found in a conventionally built house of comparable size. The system allows easy and economical modifications or even total custom design.

Cornerstone of the Justus system is a unique double-tongue-and-groove wall assembly with dovetail corner joints. Every component is pre-cut at the factory to close tolerances. The method is so precise that, after the first wall timbers are nailed into position, subsequent timbers are simply driven together, for an airtight fit, without nailing or sealant.

A Justus home can be erected faster and generally at significantly less labor costs than a similar stick-built house. It's possible and rewarding for Justus customers to construct all or part of their home themselves. Working drawings cover all phases of construction, from foundation and erection to plumbing, wiring, and heating.

There are 35 stock models in the Justus line, ranging in size from the 909-square-foot Alpental to the 2,837-square-foot McKinley. Featured here is the 1,436-square-foot Timberline, one of the many Justus chalet designs. Ideal for snow country, the Timberline can be modified to meet extreme conditions. With the Timberline's unique bay window, the view of the world outside is virtually unobstructed. Inside, the open-beam cathedral ceiling, stairway, and loft railings are a tribute to good design.

Standard package price for the three-bedroom Timberline is $33,695, F.O.B. Tacoma, Washington. The package is one of the most complete we've seen among the pre-cuts and includes everything from sub-flooring and self-sealing composition shingles to moulding and closet materials. Cedar shakes are an option at $2,000. For customers who select the option of solid cedar construction throughout, there is no paneling or painting to do because the cedar walls are the finished product.

The Justus product is marketed through a network of independent dealers located throughout the U.S. The dealer can provide complete construction assistance and follow-up after the sale, including a warrantee program.

Shipping weight for the Justus pre-cut solid cedar home is approximately 38 pounds per square foot of house, plus two pounds per square foot for a house with shakes. For the Timberline, shipping weight would be somewhere between 27 and 29 tons. (They don't call it sweat equity for nothing.) A good rule of thumb for the cost of a complete Justus turn-key house, exclusive of land, is to double the package price.

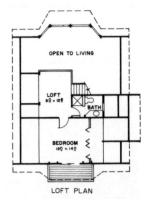

**floor plan of the Timberline**

The 4x8-inch wall timbers of the Timberline are double tongue-and-grooved and so precisely machined that they are driven together without sealant or spiking for an airtight fit.

Like all Justus solid cedar homes, the Timberline interior is as visually intriguing as the exterior—with an open, vaulted ceiling and detailed loft and stairway railings.

# Cedar Homes/The Mt. McKinley

The Mt. McKinley series, ranging from 1,128 to 1,807 square feet in floor area, is well suited to year-round or recreation use. A glass gable draws sunlight into a loft over the main-floor bedrooms of the Mt. McKinley, increasing the flexibility of the upper-level space.

Four of the 55 ways to build your dream house offered by Cedar Homes are included in the Mt. McKinley series. Well-suited to both year-round living and second-home use, the Mt. McKinley chalets range from 1,128 to 1,807 square feet in floor area. A glass gable draws sunlight into a loft over the main floor bedrooms, increasing the flexibility of the upper-level space for additional sleeping or recreation uses. The deck expanding the living and dining area beyond the view-enhancing window wall is an option.

Based on 3 × 8-inch solid cedar tongue-and-groove construction, Cedar Homes' single-wall building system is adaptable to traditional or contemporary designs, stock model or custom. The wall sections, pre-finished inside and out and pre-drilled for electrical outlets, are installed vertically. All window frames are manufactured to interlock with the wall panels. The structural soundness of the walls, made airtight with Neoprene seals between adjoining panels, is further ensured by steel tie rods.

Floor systems include 2 × 10 joists, timber girders, and tongue-and-groove plywood sub-flooring. Roof systems vary with the design series. For the Mt. McKinleys, it's beam and decking, with glu-lam or cut timber beams, 2 × 6 tongue-and-groove decking, 2-inch rigid-foam insulation and cedar shakes.

In addition to floor, wall, and roof systems, basic Cedar Homes packages include exterior and interior doors, interior partitions, wardrobes, and linen closets. Outside upper-level rear balconies are included with the two largest models in the Mt. McKinley series.

Basic package prices for the Mt. McKinleys begin at $28,800, F.O.B. Bellevue, Washington. The price includes floor and roof insulation. Cedar Homes, through its Home Interiors Department, also offers such items as kitchen cabinets, vanities, and appliances, along with prefabricated fireplaces and plumbing, heating, and electrical packages for all of its basic and custom designs.

Going further than most manufacturers of pre-cuts to minimize the hassles of new construction for the owner-builder, Cedar Homes not only delivers the materials to the job site, but inventories and lays them out for the customer's convenience. Visqueen tarps are provided to protect the building materials from the weather.

In addition to the Mt. McKinleys, Cedar Homes designs include a series incorporating a T-shaped floor plan in a chalet, California-inspired residential ramblers, split-levels, tri-level contemporaries, gambrels, square houses, and hexagons. Sizes range from 672 to 2,912 square feet.

Cedar Homes markets primarily in the 11 western states, Alaska, and Hawaii, through a network of dealers and representatives.

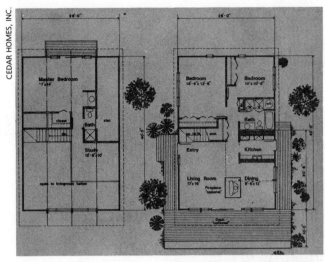

floor plan of the Mt. McKinley

A high, open-beamed ceiling adds excitement to the living room of this family home. An optional sun deck expands the living, dining, and entertainment areas beyond the view-enhancing windows.

83

# Pan Abode/The Ski Chalet

Pan Abode's Ski Chalets are constructed from solid cedar timbers that have been precision-milled for tongue-and-groove assembly with interlocking corners. The Ski Chalet II, shown here, reflects the European design and craftsmanship that go into every Pan Abode home.

A lot of European design and craftsmanship goes into every Pan Abode pre-cut cedar home—which is understandable, since Aage Jensen, who founded the company in Seattle in 1953, was a skilled cabinetmaker in his native Denmark before he turned his hand to building houses.

Pan Abode homes are designed for owner assembly. The construction method is one of the simplest of all forms of building. It is basic Scandinavian log construction with a single, broad tongue-and-groove bond and interlocking corners. The "logs," in this case, are precision milled from western red cedar timbers and measure 3 × 6 inches for single-story construction, 4 × 6 for two-story homes. Once the foundation is in place, two men can erect a Pan Abode home at an average rate of 100 square feet per day. Starter logs are the only logs that require nailing.

There are 25 stock models in the Pan Abode portfolio, including the Ski Chalet I, the Ski Chalet II, and the Ski Chalet III, offering 930, 1,145, and 1,850 square feet of living area, respectively. The exterior design of all three Ski Chalets is essentially the same. Only the dimensions are different. Inside, the front sections are much alike, too. With all three models, the living/dining area is open to a beamed cathedral ceiling and a glass front wall rising to meet the roof.

Every construction member of a Pan Abode home is individually pre-cut at the factory. Materials are inspected four times for quality and sizing during the cutting and packaging process. The pieces must match perfectly, not only in size, but in moisture content, age, and shrinkage.

In addition to the solid cedar wall members, which are utilized for interior partitioning, too, Pan Abode's pre-cut kits come complete with floor system, all windows and doors, and a complete roof system including shingles.

Stock-model kit price for the Ski Chalet I is $24,300, F.O.B. Renton, Washington. With such standard options as hand-split cedar shakes, rigid-foam roof insulation, and cedar decking, the kit price would come to roughly $27,000. If the customer chooses not to do any of the construction work himself, he can anticipate doubling the basic kit price. Most of Pan Abode's customers do construct a portion, if not all, of the home themselves, and, accordingly, they save dramatically on the ultimate cost.

Pan Abode western red cedar homes are marketed throughout the U.S. and Canada, generally through Pan Abode dealers. Other Pan Abode designs, mostly traditional, a few contemporary, range from the Mountaineer series of hideaways, with from 320 to 600 square feet, to the 2,058-square-foot Aristocrat II, which is designed to combine metropolitan family living with formal or informal entertaining.

the Ski Chalet II

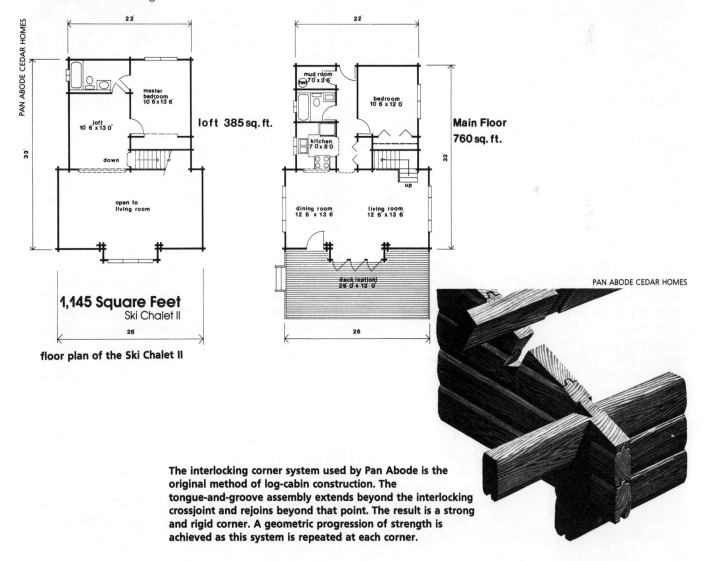

floor plan of the Ski Chalet II

The interlocking corner system used by Pan Abode is the original method of log-cabin construction. The tongue-and-groove assembly extends beyond the interlocking crossjoint and rejoins beyond that point. The result is a strong and rigid corner. A geometric progression of strength is achieved as this system is repeated at each corner.

# Wickes Lumber/The Lake Haus

The Lake Haus, with its rustic chalet styling, is one of three models in Wickes' Haus series. Like all Wickes' family of affordable homes, it comes with wall sections, gable ends, trusses, and partitions largely pre-assembled for easy erection.

One of the big names in "affordable" housing, Wickes Lumber designs its houses for easy construction by non-professionals. Wall sections, gable ends, stairs, and partitions all come pre-assembled. And once you've completed the basic shell, Wickes allows you to stretch out your housing investment over a period of time by offering you a selection of interior finishing packages that you can install at your own pace.

For example, there are packages available which provide you with plans, instructions, and all materials for installing plumbing, heating, and electrical systems in your home. There's an insulation package, plus complete interior finish packages which you choose room by room to suit your taste and budget. Every buyer of a Wickes kit house also gets a copy of How to Build Your Own Home, a very useful 336-page book by Robert C. Reschke covering all aspects of home building.

The Haus series, with distinctive Bavarian styling, is one of 10 Wickes' design series. Other series cover everything from New England salt-box to contemporary bi-level designs, from year-round residences to vacation hideaways in the country. The Lake Haus, shown here, measures 24 × 30 feet. In addition, there's a half-loft with a balcony rail that overlooks the living room. The loft easily can be converted into a master bedroom with bath and walk-in closet.

Large families can "stretch" the living space of the Lake Haus by any increment of two feet, front or rear, at the time of construction. Wickes' system of interchangeable door and window modules lets you choose from four styles of front-door-and-window configurations. There's also a handy service entrance which opens directly into the utility room.

Each model in the Haus series comes with all materials for completing the basic shell and can be built on a slab, crawl space, basement, or pier-and-beam foundation.

The basic shell package for the 24 × 30-foot Lake Haus with half-loft costs $7,799, F.O.B. Saginaw, Michigan. With floor deck (over crawl space), plumbing, wiring, insulation, forced-air heating, trim, standard interior finish package, and kitchen cabinets, total package cost would come to around $16,800. Even this might be deferred on Wickes' time-payment plan. The rest is sweat equity.

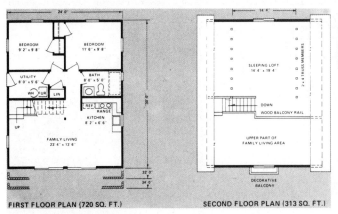

**floor plan of the Lake Haus**

Wickes' houses are designed for easy construction. Instead of just a truckload of pre-cut lumber, much of the Lake Haus is delivered to the site in pre-assembled sections.

All wall sections are numbered. You start by placing the first section at a corner and work around the building. Interior partitions are worked in as you proceed with the outside walls.

**exploded view of the Lake Haus construction**

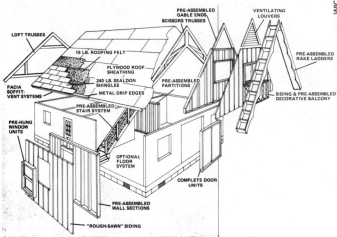

There are four front-window-and-door treatment options with the Lake Haus.

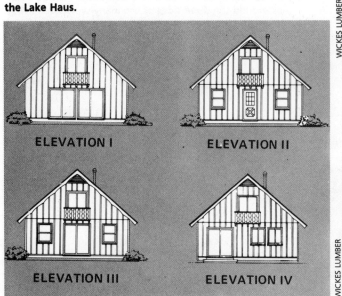

Siding comes in 4-foot-wide sheets and is nailed directly to the studs.

Trusses are positioned, braced, and nailed. Note that the truss includes the knee wall and floor joist built in to frame and support the loft area.

Erected in Anchorage, Alaska, this six-sided Lindal home is neatly divided in halves. The view-oriented "half" is entirely devoted to a wide-open living area, and the other "half" contains kitchen, dining room, and bedrooms. A large deck wraps around the three sides of the many-windowed living area. Imagine the drama . . . and fun . . . of living in a home like this!

It takes a "round" house to take full advantage of settings such as this. Here, the owner has clustered three of Rondesics' polyhouses to give him everything he wanted in a home.

# POLYGONS & ROUND HOUSES

Octagonal houses became a fad in the 1840s when a popular author of the time, Orson Squire Fowler, who wrote about marital problems and phrenology, expounded the theory that the eight-sided design would significantly improve the health of the house's occupants. Today, octagons are back in vogue—not for any health or mystical reasons, but simply because, as more and more families are finding out, the octagon and other "round houses," the popular appellation for all polygonal designs, take better advantage of most sites than do a mere four walls.

Polygons begin with five-sided figures, but we're not aware of any pentagons in kit form. There are, however, some noteworthy six- and eight-sided designs, one of which sits on a pedestal and is fondly referred to as "the treehouse." And if it's "round" you want, there's a 28-sided panelized design, offered by Pacific Panel Homes. There's also the Meyer Round, which is truly round. Even the doors and windows are curved.

With more than four walls, a choice site is a must. The whole idea is to take maximum advantage of the views, whether in an alpine, wooded, beach, or lakeside setting. Most polygonal designs incorporate more glass than wood in the exterior walls and can provide an unobstructed view from virtually every part of the house. Where privacy is desired, the use of glass is more limited.

The frame of a polyhouse is totally self-supporting. Roofs are vaulted and no load-bearing interior walls are needed. You have complete freedom of design inside. Exterior walls generally are assembled from a selection of factory-produced panels, with doors and windows installed. The panels provide a finished exterior, insulated core, and finished interior wall all in one. Some of the building systems require little more than attaching panels to a frame that simply bolts together.

These many-sided houses can be erected on any type of foundation. With a radial-beam floor system, offered by some manufacturers, the structure can be supported by piers or poles and made to straddle a brook, cling to a mountainside, or sit over a boulder.

Where more living space is needed, two or more polyhouses can be clustered, or a smaller unit, accessible via a walkway, can serve as a satellite bedroom or playroom. You could even begin with the smaller unit and grow later. A rectangular wing is another design possibility, either initially or as an add-on. Some units also are stackable.

In finishing the interior of a polygon, acute angles can be avoided by installing divider walls perpendicular to exterior walls rather than bringing them out from corners. Though bedrooms are irregularly shaped, there's usually ample room for furniture placement and closet space. Just don't sub-divide a small polyhouse to excess.

If you've already decided that a log house is the answer to your dream, you still can build a polygon. At least three log manufacturers include polygonal designs in their log-house portfolios. Authentic Homes offers a two-story hexagon based on the Navaho hogan. National Log Construction Company has 10-sided "Early American" round and oval designs. And Lodge Logs by MacGregor covers still another option with a 16-sided solar house.

The Topsider sits on a pedestal—and rightfully so. It's one of the most popular houses ever offered in prefab form.

One of Forest Homes' four hexagons, the 1,254-square-foot Mandalay can be purchased as a shell kit for about one-third the price you'd pay for the three-bedroom house if totally constructed on your lot by a builder.

AUTHENTIC HOMES CORP.

If you're torn between a log house and a polygon, Authentic Homes' Navaho, which can be built as a one-story house with two bedrooms, or a two-story house with three or four bedrooms, could give you the best of both worlds.

An excellent design for that suburban hillside lot, the 28-sided Lakeview takes advantage of the scenery with the panoramic view that circular living offers. Pacific Panel Homes' three-bedroom, 2 1/2-bath design with central spiral staircase offers formal or informal living to suit your style.

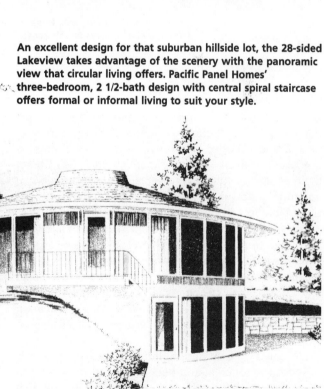

PACIFIC PANEL HOMES

# Topsider Vacation Homes/The Topsider

The unique Topsider, adaptable to any climate, is becoming a familiar sight from the Florida Keys to the Pacific Northwest. As both vacation and full-time residences, they're grown-up answers to kids' dreams.

Developers looking for something new and different gave the Topsider, the prefab-set-on-a-pedestal, its first big boost. There are sizable colonies of the "treehouses" near Disney World, in Florida, and at Big Canoe, a 5,400-acre haven north of Atlanta. They also attract their share of long-stay visitors to resort/residential communities at Hilton Head Island, South Carolina, and Cape Eleuthera in the Bahamas.

For a while, in the early '70s, seven out of every 10 Topsiders were being put up by resort-area developers. Now it's individual buyers who account for the bulk of the business, and the unique structures, adaptable to any climate, are becoming a familiar sight from the Florida Keys to the Pacific Northwest. As both vacation and full-time residences, they're grown-up answers to kids' dreams.

Designed by Guy Bartoli, the eight-sided Topsider is raised on a concrete-and-steel-reinforced pedestal and sheathed with insulated glass on all sides for minimal site disturbance and an unobstructed view from every part of the house. It is adaptable to almost any site condition and blends into the natural landscape as if it grew out of the ground. The units are insulated and stressed to withstand winds of up to 140 mph.

There are four models of the Topsider and two models of the Mini-Topsider. The Mini-Topsider has the same features as the full-size, 33-foot-diameter Topsider, but with less floor space. The diameter of the Mini is 25-feet-8-inches, for 473 square feet on the main level. The basic two-bedroom, two-bath Topsider has 800 square feet of living area on the lofty main level, plus a heated utility room with another 100 square feet in the pedestal base. Model 102 has in addition a 100-square-foot lower entry.

The Topsider structural system consists of a central steel support column, pre-cut timber floor trusses, and pre-assembled roof trusses and exterior posts, with all necessary steel connectors and bolts. Floor and roof panels are pre-cut and fully insulated. The roof panels also provide the pre-finished ceiling.

The exterior wall system consists of eight large wall frames and eight corner panels. Two of the wall frames have pre-hung entry doors. To be fitted into the wall frames are 16 panels of insulated glass and six solid insulated panels. The corner panels are complete with jalousie windows, screens, and storms.

Kit price for this home-with-a-360-degree-view varies depending on model and choice of options. Figure at least $21,000 (F.O.B. Yadkinville, North Carolina) for the larger model. The components supplied include two complete bathrooms and kitchen cabinetry, plus the partitions and closets necessary to divide the house into a two-bedroom, two-bath plan.

Roofing shingles are not included. A steel spiral stairway is another option. The staircase and enclosed lower entry assembly add about $1,400 to the base price. One alternative to an inside staircase would be an outside wooden stairway leading to an optional cantilevered deck.

With the cantilevered construction, this is not an easy house for the inexperienced builder. When Topsider does the job, it takes an experienced six-man crew about 10 working days to assemble the house after the pedestal foundation has been poured.

**The structural system of the Topsider consists of a central steel support column and rigid bolted trusses. Much of the roof-truss system comes pre-assembled with bolted steel connections attached. The floor-truss system is assembled from pre-drilled, construction-grade timbers.**

**floor plan and elevation of the Topsider 102**

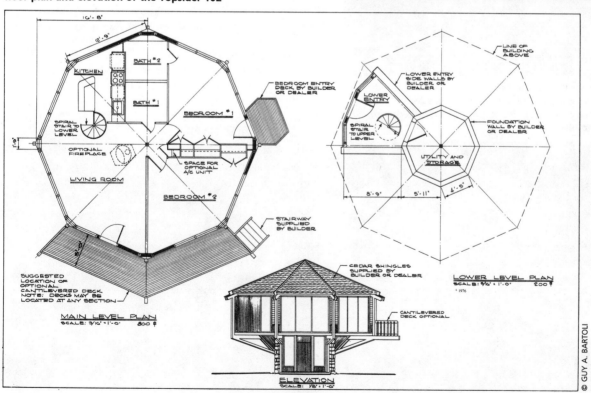

The Topsider as it leaves the factory. The entire house package, with the exception of the insulated glass and the bathrooms, which are shipped separately, can be carried in one enclosed trailer.

Interior views of a Topsider. Components supplied include bathrooms and kitchen cabinetry, plus the partitions and closets necessary to divide the house into a two-bedroom, two-bathroom plan.

A steel spiral staircase is a Topsider option. The staircase and enclosed lower entry add about $1,400 to the base price. One alternative would be an outside wooden stairway leading to an optional cantilevered deck.

The Topsider is adaptable to almost any site condition and blends into the natural landscape as if it grew out of the ground.

# Rondesics Homes/Round Houses

The Rondesics home suits any terrain, even rugged, untouched land that is worthless as a site for most homes. Designed not only for piers and steel pilings, it can also be built on a concrete slab, with a crawl space or with a full basement.

The Rondesics "round" house is basically a panelized redwood structure with a pre-cut roof system. The exterior walls or sides of these structures are made up of from eight to 15 same-size prefabricated panels—some solid, some with windows, and some with doors. Both structural and full packages, including interior finishing materials and appliances, are offered for five models, ranging from 336 to 1,165 square feet in floor area. Units of any size can function separately. But flexibility is the word here. Any two or more Rondesics units can be joined. Like sizes can be stacked to double the area under one roof. Or you can stack two and connect satellite units to them.

You have the same flexibility with the interior. Dividing walls are not load bearing. You can arrange the interior as you like. The system is designed to accommodate all kinds of options, from a steeper-pitched roof to thicker-insulated walls to extra decking. Two sections of redwood decking come with the structural package, but additional sections can be ordered. You could surround the house with decking. It's all up to you.

Upkeep is kept to a minimum with rough-sawn, premium-grade redwood siding, the beauty of which is enhanced through natural weathering. And to capture the best view of the great outdoors, you can choose from a variety of window-wall and door sections. With Rondesics' large window panels, the view can be virtually from floor to ceiling. Privacy is ensured where desired with solid-panel walls.

Rondesics will work directly with the customer or his contractor, but does not recommend that customers unfamiliar with standard building techniques attempt to erect the structure on their own. There are many opportunities, though, once the shell is completed, for the owner to participate in the finishing of the house. As a rule, most customers just buy the structural package from Rondesics, with the interior finishing materials, appliances, and the like obtained by the customer or his contractor from local sources.

The dwelling suits almost any terrain and little has to be done to accommodate it. Designed not only for piers and steel pilings, a Rondesics home can be built on a concrete slab, with a crawl space, or over a full basement.

The R-8 (eight sides) efficiency, with a diameter of 21-feet-7-inches and 336 square feet of floor area, is Rondesics' compact model and is most often used as a guest house or private retreat off the beaten track. When connected to a larger unit, the R-8 makes an ideal family room, studio, or master bedroom suite. If you require two bedrooms, the 12-sided, 735-square-foot R-12 could be the answer. It accommodates two bedrooms, one bath, a kitchen and dining area, a living room, and plenty of closet space. The 15-sided, 1,165-square-foot R-15 is the big one. It easily allows for three bedrooms and two baths.

Prices range from $9,064 for the R-8 structural package ($12,186, full package) to $19,606 for the R-15 ($27,391, full package), F.O.B. Asheville, North Carolina. These prices do not include erection of the structure.

Structural packages include floor beams, pre-insulated floor panels, redwood skirtboards, two sections of redwood deck with railings, underlayment, pre-insulated wall sections, exterior doors, complete structural roof system including pre-cut rafters and sheathing, compression ring, roof peak vent, and all hardware, spikes, and nails needed to erect the shell.

Full packages include the structural package plus interior partition framing lumber, interior paneling, sheetrock for ceilings, pre-hung interior doors, bi-fold closet doors, interior trim, kitchen cabinets and counters, stainless-steel sink, refrigerator, range, bathroom fixtures, baseboard electric heating elements, and floor tile.

The Rondesics' round houses are marketed through a network of builder/dealers mostly east of the Mississippi.

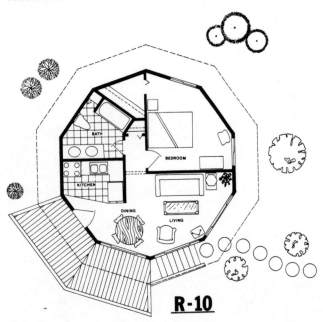

**floor plan of the Rondesics R-10**

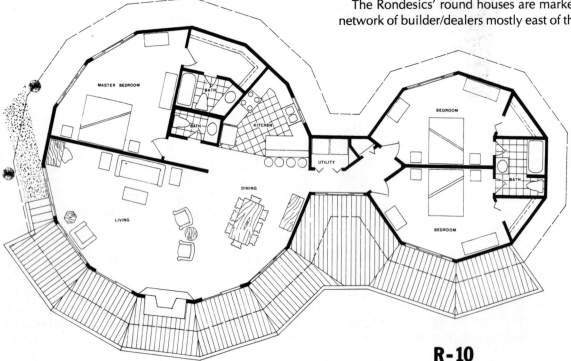

**R-15**

**R-10**

the Rondesics R-10 connected to the R-15

RONDESICS HOMES CORP.

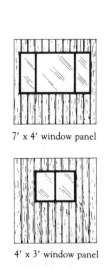

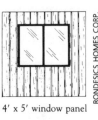
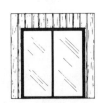

7' x 4' window panel   7' x 5'4" window panel   4' x 5' window panel

4' x 3' window panel   2' x 2' window panel   Sliding glass door panel

Door panel   Fireplace panel   Solid wall panel

To capture the best view of the great outdoors and provide privacy where desired, you can choose from a wide variety of window-wall and door sections. The exterior finish is rough-sawn redwood siding.

For those who build in the mountains, 6-inch wall framing with thicker insulation is an option. Decking is another popular option. Although two sections of redwood decking come with a Rondesics home, additional sections can be specified.

The Rondesics design creates not only more floor space, but exposes less exterior surface to the elements than conventional rectangular construction.

Each of the five different-size Rondesics structures can function separately as a home. But flexibility is the word to remember. Like sizes can be stacked, and any two or more sizes can be connected for additional living space. The combinations are limitless.

# W. H. Porter/The Port Six

With the Port-R-Span building system, it takes two people just a few days to erect a Port Six shell on a prepared foundation.

The six-sided Port Six is a cleverly engineered structure that utilizes prefabricated building panels—in both the wall and roof systems—to provide a weatherproof exterior finish, a rigid-foam insulating core, and an attractive interior finish all in one step. Developed by W. H. Porter, Inc., the Port-R-Span building system is so simple that a Port Six can be erected on a previously prepared foundation by two men in just a few days.

The key to the Port Six is a high-strength, lightweight tubular-steel frame that simply bolts together. With pre-drilled holes and factory-attached channels, bolts, and end plates, the framing goes together quickly and precisely. The entire knocked-down frame—columns, trusses, rafters, tension members, and compression ring—can be carried to the construction site in one load by a pickup truck. The heaviest single part weighs only 146 pounds.

Once the frame is up, the prefabricated roof panels are installed, followed by the wall panels. The wall panels are held at the top by a panel retainer, and after each sidewall is completed, they are screwed to a base plate. The side edges of each panel are recessed for rigid 2 × 4 vertical splining.

The Port Six is offered in two sizes: with 18- or 22-foot sidewalls. Floor areas are 880 and 1,304 square feet, respectively. For residential or vacation use, it can be built atop a concrete slab, over a crawl space or basement, or with the columns extended as piers (for a sloped building site).

This is a shell of a house. The hexagon shape, with a vaulted cathedral ceiling leading up to a center skylight, allows for full use of the interior space with no inside support walls. The interior arrangement is entirely up to the owner. Since the interior arrangement will, to some degree, dictate exterior door and window placement, the buyer of a Port Six should lay out a floor plan before making his wall-panel selections. Room divisions at the corners of the hexagon should be avoided since a division at this point makes a tight angle resulting in lost space.

There are 18 different panels—from solid panels in 1-, 2-, 3-, and 4-foot widths to 14- and 16-foot-wide sliding-glass-door panels. Other choices include panels with single, double, and triple windows, both awning and casement type.

The kit price of a Port Six will vary depending on the wall panels selected. The basic kit includes only the framing, insulated roof, and skylight. For the Model 18, the price of this package is $8,295. Shingles and roofing felt are an option at $465. Figure roughly $5,000 for the

108 feet of wall panels needed to enclose the Model 18—or a total price of around $14,000, F.O.B. Holland, Michigan. Base price for the Model 22 is $12,140. With shingles ($650) and a typical selection of wall panels, the total package price would come to approximately $20,000.

The Port Six frame-and-roof package can be ordered without a selection of panels to allow owner-builders to incorporate local materials such as adobe or brick into the sidewall design.

art showing various adaptations of the Port Six

floor plan of the Port Six model 18

**The frame of the Port Six supports the entire building. There are no interior bearing walls, which provides the possibility to relocate interior walls in the future. Frame members are pre-engineered to go together fast.**

**Wall panels, installed with rigid 2 x 4 vertical splines, provide finished exterior, insulating core, and finished interior wall all in one.**

**The shape of the Port Six, with the vaulted ceiling leading to a center compression ring/skylight, allows you to partition the interior as you choose.**

# Meyer Round Structures/The Meyer Round

Pre-cut and panelized for easy construction, the Meyer Round is truly circular. Even the exterior doors and windows are curved.

Most so-called "round" houses actually are polygons, made up of a limited number of straight-wall sections or sides. But the Meyer Round, using a curved, extruded-aluminum sill-and-header system, is truly circular. Even the exterior doors and windows are curved. It's the only truly circular design we know of available in kit form for do-it-yourself construction.

There are one-, two-, three-, four-, and five-bedroom versions of the Meyer Round, with from one to three bathrooms, depending on the size of the house. Built with rooms radiating out from a central core, the long, space-wasting halls found in most rectilinear houses have been eliminated. Diameters run from 30 to 61 feet and square footage from 735 to 2,922.

The design and construction of the Meyer Round incorporate pre-cut and panelized parts. Most of the construction materials, beginning with the wedge-shaped sub-floor panels, are specialty items milled or fabricated by Meyer Round Structures.

The materials package for the shell is delivered to the site after completion of the sub-structure through the radial-beam floor system. The exterior walls are formed with curved, 4 × 8-foot, prefabricated post-and-rib sections to which paneling is attached by the builder. Insulation and gypsum board on the inside face complete the structural wall. The curved core wall is formed with gypsum board applied to both faces of the post-and-rib system.

All exterior doors and windows are curved. Windows are aluminum-framed with acrylic lites. The curved panes are shatter-resistant and have a greater insulation value than glass. They can be ordered tinted to reduce glare or solar heat transmittance. Roof-system beams are tapered, sloping to the central core. A special snow-load roof system is an option.

Heating and plumbing can be located in the central core for shortened heat and water runs. The core also could be used to provide access to a spiral staircase to a lower level. Plexiglass bubble skylights are included to brighten the core and inside bathrooms.

Minimum shell package prices begin at $11,520, F.O.B. Hayward, California, for the 30-foot-diameter Meyer Round. An interior partitions-and-doors package is an option at $1,487.

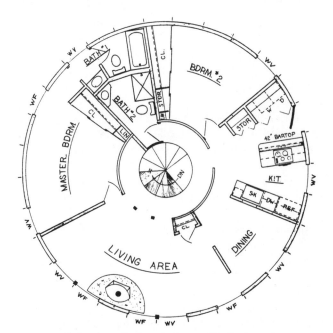

floor plan of a two-bedroom Meyer Round

Exterior walls are formed with curved, prefabricated post-and-rib sections to which exterior paneling is attached by the builder.

Insulation and gypsum board on the inside face complete the structural wall

Curved windowpanes are acrylic and may be ordered tinted to reduce glare or solar heat transmittance. They have a greater insulation value than glass.

# G. L. Industries/Hexagons

**For close encounters with the great outdoors in a wooded setting, the many-windowed hexagon is a design that's hard to fault.**

Pre-cut and partially panelized packages for constructing hexagons measuring from 12 to 30 feet per side—or from 374 to 2,338 square feet in floor areas—are offered by G. L. Industries. The buyer may purchase the building system package to erect himself (it is designed for the do-it-yourselfer) or contract to have all or part of the structure built by a professional crew.

With such G. L. I. options as a radial-beam floor-framing system, the hexagon can be set atop piers or poles to adapt to a sloping site or other problem terrain without disturbing the ecology. The standard floor system is parallel-joists-and-girder for construction over a crawl space or basement. Sub-flooring is 1½-inch tongue-and-groove boards or 1⅛-inch tongue-and-groove plywood. The buildings are free-vaulting, with an open-beam ceiling.

Each framing member, precision-cut and pre-drilled, comes ready for assembly. The Douglas fir posts, headers, and roof beams are simply bolted together, like a giant Erector Set, to form a totally self-supporting, rigid skeleton to which wall panels and roof decking are attached. Wall sections are 4 × 8-foot redwood panels and frames with pre-engineered window openings. Sliding-glass doors, solid wall panels, and window panels can be placed in virtually any sequence in the hex to take maximum advantage of the views or to provide privacy.

The panels are braced with 2 × 4 studding, and the inside face is left open to allow for the installation of water lines, wiring, and insulation at the owner's convenience after the shell has been closed to the weather. The roof system includes 2-inch tongue-and-groove decking, rigid-foam insulation, and shingles or shakes.

Among the options: a cupola, approximately 6 feet per side for the standard model, 8 feet per side for the deluxe model. The radial-beam floor system is available with extensions to accommodate sections of deck.

Kit prices for the shell components of a G. L. I. hexagon range from $12 to $15 per square foot—or from $18,000 to $22,500, F.O.B. San Jose, California, for a 24-foot hexagon.

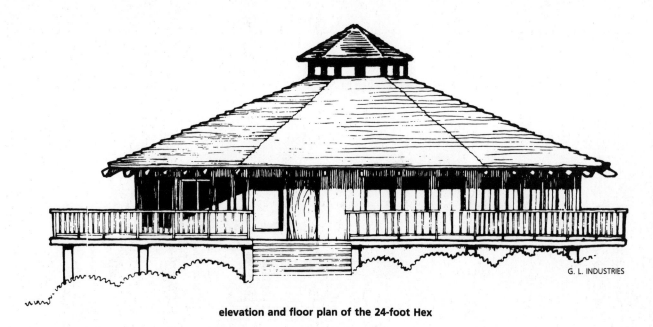

**elevation and floor plan of the 24-foot Hex**

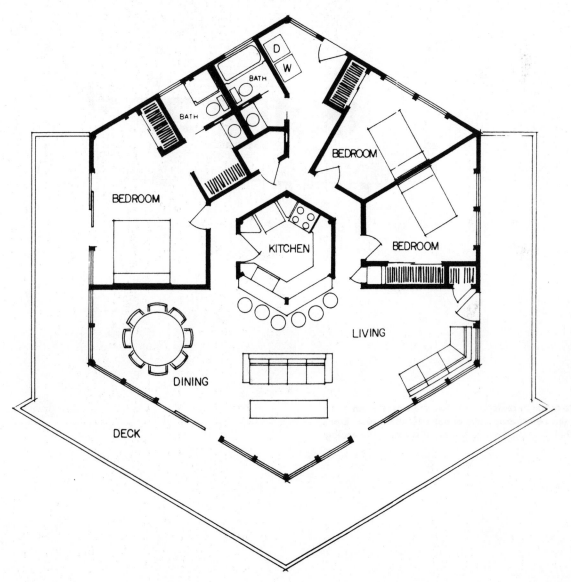

103

With GLI's optional radial-beam, floor-framing system, the hexagon can be set atop piers or poles to adapt to a sloping site or other problem terrain without disturbing the ecology.

An isometric view of GLI's 24-foot (per side) Hex with 1,496 square feet of floor area. The "carousel kitchen" is a feature of many of GLI's designs.

# TRADITIONALS

Unconventional housing styles seldom find acceptance in built-up communities. Zoning laws, restrictive covenants, and the banker's reluctance to finance any but "safe" houses that can easily be sold or rented see to that. If you are planning to build in suburbia, odds are that the house will be of a traditional design, whether that's your first choice or not.

"Traditional" covers everything from Cape Cods and two-story Colonials to one-story "ranchers" and split-levels. It might seem a little strange to think of a type of housing that didn't become popular until after World War II as traditional rather than contemporary, but that's the case with the split-level, which is being succeeded even now by the bi-level, also known as the raised ranch or split-entry.

The one-story ranch (originally named "the rambling ranch") is still the most common type of detached housing being built in most areas of the country. Prior to the 1960s, the 1½-story Cape Cod style was the national favorite, and before that, from pre-Revolutionary days until the 1920s, it was the two-story Colonial.

While one-floor living may be easier, there are definite advantages in building up instead of out. The house can be built on a smaller lot, a very important consideration in urban and suburban areas. With twice the living space on the same foundation and only half as much roofing required, construction costs for an owner-built two-story house can be as much as 30 percent less per square foot than for a one-story house of equal floor area. With two separate floors, leisure and living areas are downstairs, with sleeping areas upstairs for total privacy.

Many traditional two-story designs are difficult to expand. They don't lend themselves to add-ons without corrupting the lines. But one solution is to build a large house initially, live in comfort on the finished first floor, and finish off the second floor as family and/or income grow. This also is a popular way to go with the 1½-story Cape Cods.

"One-story ranch" describes a wide variety of one-story designs, including bungalows, largely adapted to

This "Cape Cod" has the look of an authentic antique, built by New Englanders 200 or more years ago. The four-bedroom Newbury is understandably one of the Northern Homes' most popular houses.

Contributing to the popularity of ranch-style houses like the Marshfield is the "no-stairs" convenience, a time and energy saver. For others, when it's time to expand, a full basement can be ready and waiting for the shop, laundry, or den.

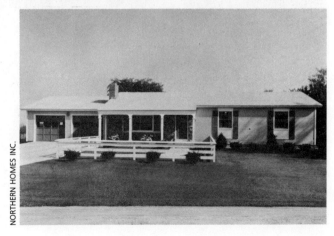

107

indoor/outdoor life-styles. Often built over a crawl space rather than a full basement, they're among the easiest of all houses to build for primary year-round use. The low height simplifies construction. But there are a couple of kickers. With the ratio of walls, roof, and foundation to total living area, the rancher, on a square-footage basis, is costlier to build than most other designs. On the same basis, ranch models also tend to be more expensive to heat and cool.

Though most are built on level ground today, the split-level was conceived as the solution to a sloping lot. It has many of the advantages of the ranch, with most of the features of the two-story house. With floors halfway between other floors, only a few steps separate levels. The design, however, does ensure privacy and is practical for the busy, active family.

**Available in 20- and 24-foot widths in any length that is a multiple of 4 feet, Crestline/Wideline TimberLodges are basically ranch-style units with 4-foot modular post-and-beam construction, glu-lam trussed rafters, and exposed-redwood roof deck.**

The new trend is toward bi-levels that elevate the basement several feet, add lots of glass, and use the basement for full-time living. The foyer of most houses of this type is split, with a half-flight of stairs leading up and a half-flight leading down, from grade, or a few steps above.

A majority of the designs offered by the shell-builders come under the "traditional" umbrella. Depending on zoning and building codes as they apply to non-professional construction, you may have no choice but to go to a shell-builder and have at least this much of your house erected by a crew of professionals. The usual arrangement with this type of construction, where codes permit and the owner has the option, is to have the builder leave the interior, or some portion of it, for the owner to finish.

Geography, as well as the "age" of the design, often dictates what is traditional in housing. Forest Homes' Pueblo Three could be very "contemporary" in New England, but in the Southwest, few houses could be more traditional. The Pueblo Three is from Forest Homes' desert-style homes collection.

FOREST HOMES

RIDGE HOMES

A two-story Dutch Colonial with luxury features at an affordable price, the Shelbourne is one of the many traditional designs offered by Ridge Homes. Ridge's pre-cut custom homes are semi-constructed on the customer's lot—and over 30,000 homeowners can testify that Ridge's Finish-It-Yourself building program works.

NORTHERN HOMES, INC.

The authentic look of this New England colonial, the Ben Franklin, from Northern Homes' Americana Collection, is captured in its narrow clapboard siding, multiple-light windows, square chimney, and symmetrical entry. Flexibility is built in and stems from the New England custom of starting with a minimal structure and adding wings as needed.

# Northern Homes/The Sherbrooke

**The interior of the Sherbrooke is everything the exterior hints at, with a floor plan that is one of the most workable we've seen in a ranch.**

Northern Homes has made its reputation along the eastern seaboard with its traditional designs. Its Americana Collection of traditionals are so accurately reproduced that they look like antiques. There are 31 traditional designs in this manufacturer's portfolio, ranging in size from the 912-square-foot Rockport, an economy version of the ranch house, to the 3,502-square-foot Ethan Allen, a salt-box with true proportions and honest detail (you can almost see the British mustering in front of the house).

Shown here is the Sherbrooke, a ranch house with a New England accent. There are three bedrooms and 1,184 square feet of living space. The floor plan is one of the most workable we've seen in a ranch. A 12 × 19-foot living room with lots of wall space permits a wide variety of furniture arrangements. The dining room adjoining the kitchen means dining can be either formal, or the room can be an informal adjunct to the kitchen, depending on how it's decorated. On the other side of the kitchen is a separate laundry room with its own closet.

The three bedrooms in this house are also arranged for versatility. The bedroom off the living room is well located for use as a combination study/guest room. The master bedroom has two exposures for lots of light and fresh air. The third bedroom, also a corner room, is at the back of the house, a nice quiet location for a child's room.

The Sherbrooke's attached garage offers a bonus for the man of the house. At the back he will have room for a shop or a storage area for garden equipment. Doors into the house and to the outside make this space easy and convenient to use even when the car is garaged.

About 60 percent of Northern Homes' sales are for contractor construction right up to the moving-in stage. True do-it-yourselfers, however, represent about 10 percent of Northern's customers. Another 30 percent do some of the work themselves, after the shell has been erected. Northern Homes' dealership network extends from Maine to Ohio and to North Carolina. Most of the dealers have a crew or crews at their call who will do all or any part of the construction the customer wishes.

Northern's customers have the advantage of both the prefab method of construction and custom-building techniques. Using only western kiln-dried lumber for its structural systems, all building materials are prepared in the plant and are shipped to the site ready for assembly.

The packages are unusually complete and include the floor system, pre-cut exterior and interior wall materials, panelized gables, pre-cut rafters or trusses, roof sheathing and shingles, windows and pre-hung doors, underlayment, insulation, trim, and hardware. For the Sherbrooke, the kit price comes to $18,316, F.O.B. Hudson Falls, New York, or Chambersberg, Pennsylvania.

A do-it-yourselfer could probably save 20 to 25 percent of the retail value of a completed Northern home.

With more than 25,000 homes behind them, Northern Homes has had a lot of experience in translating dreams into reality. The company has skilled draftsmen on hand to adapt any of its designs to a customer's specific needs—from adding on a wing to incorporating an antique threshold.

In addition to its many traditional designs, Northern offers seven contemporary designs, a 17-model Pacesetter "economy" series, and 12 vacation-type homes in its All Season Homes series.

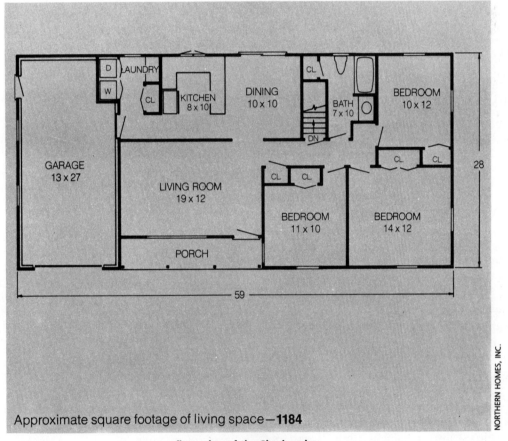

Approximate square footage of living space—1184

**floor plan of the Sherbrooke**

# Timberpeg/Traditional Gambrel

The large center chimney, the dormers, and divided-light, double-hung windows identify this as a traditional gambrel design. The rustic post-and-beam interior and the traditional exterior of pine boards and battens combine to offer the honest beauty of days gone by.

America's master barn and bridge builders made their reputations with post-and-beam framing in the eighteenth and nineteenth centuries. The sound construction method is no less valid for today's Timberpeg homes.

The frame of a Timberpeg house is built of solid eastern white pine timbers secured one to another by interlocking mortise-and-tenon joints pegged with oak trunnels (or tree-nails). With the main framing members measuring 8 × 12, 6 × 8, and 6 × 6, collarties and angle bracing measuring 6 × 6 and 4 × 6, it is a frame that is built to last . . . and last . . . and last.

When the Timberpeg frame has been erected, squared up, all pegs hammered into place, and wedges driven home to snug the sill and purlin joints, the walls and roof are installed. The wall system begins with specially milled, kiln-dried, 1 × 8-inch tongue-and-groove pine boards, applied to the outside of the frame, either vertically or diagonally. This not only creates an uninterrupted thermal barrier, but provides a handsome interior finish that blends beautifully with the rugged, exposed frame.

The next wall material is 2-inch Thermax insulation board. Then comes a grid of 1 × 4 strapping to create an air space which gives additional insulating value to the total wall system. The exterior wall surface is 1 × 12 rough-sawn white pine siding, installed vertically, with the rough-sawn face exposed. All vertical joints are then covered with 1 × 3 pine battens before stain of the owner's selection is applied. The completed wall sandwich provides an insulation value in excess of R-22.

The roof system is much like the wall construction, with 1 × 8-inch pine decking, 2-inch insulation board, a layer of roofing felt, 1 × 4 shingle ribs, and then hand-split cedar shakes, for an approximate insulation value of R-23.

Featured here, with gambrel roof, large center chimney, dormers, and double-hung windows with divided light grilles, is one of Timberpeg's two traditional gambrel models. Overall dimensions of the house, the interior of which can be made traditional or contemporary, formal or relaxed, according to the preference of the owner, are 24 × 36 feet, for 1,728 square feet of floor area.

Price of the component package for the model shown, not including materials for the garage, is $24,000, F.O.B. Claremont, New Hampshire. The kit includes the mortised-and-tenoned framing timbers, oak pegs, all necessary lumber for interior and exterior siding and ceilings, hand-split cedar shakes, insulation for walls and roof, upper-level floor decking, all nails, windows, sliding-glass doors, pre-hung exterior doors, and skylights. Smooth, V-jointed 1 × 6 pine boards or narrow clapboards are available as an alternate exterior siding.

In addition to the traditional gambrels, Timberpeg offers two contemporary gambrel designs, two contemporary salt-box designs, and a barn house design. There also are four Cluster Sheds (see page 144), small buildings designed to be used individually or grouped in various ways to create attractive and efficient living space, and eight models that include combinations of Cluster Sheds and the larger Timberpeg designs.

Many of Timberpeg's network of authorized dealers are experienced Timberpeg builders or are affiliated with independent contracting firms. You may do it yourself, use one of Timberpeg's dealer-contractors, or select another builder in your area.

**Few houses being built today have a frame as rugged as that of a Timberpeg house. The solid eastern white pine timbers are secured one to another by interlocking mortise-and-tenon joints pegged with oak trunnels.**

**the Traditional Gambrel without the garage and the nontraditional patio doors.**

**floor plan of Timberpeg's Traditional Gambrel Design #366**

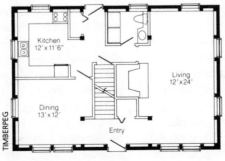

**First Floor**

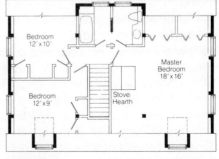

**Second Floor**

113

# American Timber Homes/The Country Squire

**The massive log trusses and cathedral ceiling of the Country Squire set the mood for a relaxing way of life.**

Designed for year-round relaxed living, American Timber Homes' sturdy Country Squire has a maintenance-free cedar exterior and a warm, friendly interior, with timber trusses, real wood paneling, and a cathedral ceiling setting the mood. The Country Squire is from American Timber's one-story log-truss series. It can be built with 960, 1,040, or 1,248 square feet of floor area and easily accommodates three bedrooms.

American Timber's building system features panelized walls and a roof system supported by hand-hewn-log or dimensional-lumber trusses. The trusses (balsam fir) are all functional parts of the building. There are no fake beams here. All exterior walls are sided with rough-sawn northern white cedar, which requires no paint, stain, or upkeep. The wall system, with 2 × 6 studs standard, consists of 8-foot-tall panels manufactured in 8-, 9-, and 10-foot widths.

Floor-system materials are not included in the package supplied by American Timber Homes. Joists and sub-flooring should be in place atop the masonry foundation when the building package is delivered. Plans are provided for foundation and joist systems. The standard Timber Homes package includes log trusses, porch and exterior deck materials, prefabricated wall panels, 2-inch tongue-and-groove roof decking, interior paneling, and partitions per plan. Wood-framed windows are double glazed and exterior doors are insulated. All materials supplied contribute to super-tight construction.

The roof trusses of the Country Squire are supported by 4 × 6 pilasters built into the ends of panels that are to be fastened together to support the trusses. Interior and exterior roof caps are used to connect the panels to the roof deck, which also serves as the finished ceiling. The panels themselves are assembled with 1-inch kiln-dried cedar siding over building felt and half-inch sheathing, all of which is fastened to 2 × 6 framing. With the interior finish wall of tongue-and-groove pine installed (after in-the-wall plumbing, wiring, and insulation have been taken care of), the wall is over seven inches thick, providing excellent insulation and structural strength.

Price of the basic kit for the 24 × 40 Country Squire is $26,418. The price includes delivery from Escanaba, Michigan, to sites accessible by semi-trailer truck in most states east of the Mississippi and a few to the west.

In addition to the log-truss series, American Timber Homes offers year-round houses in a wide variety of architectural styles, including chalet, split-level, Dutch Colonial, and contemporary, plus a solar series (see page 150) produced for Solartran. To help customers get the floor plan and design that fits their needs to a T, a custom-design service is also offered.

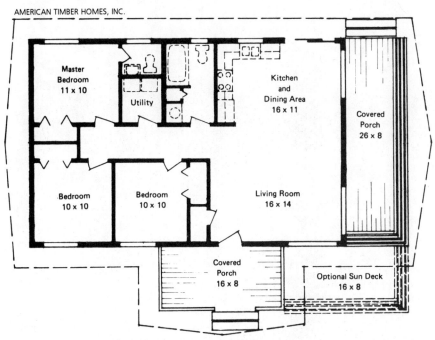

**floor plan of the Country Squire, with three bedrooms, 1 1/2 baths**

**The Country Squire can provide the relaxed atmosphere of a vacation retreat year-round in a primary residence.**

# Miles Homes/The Mt. Vernon

The Mt. Vernon, somewhat modified here, is a classic colonial, well suited for larger families on a limited budget. It is not untypical of the more than 12,000 homes that have been built by do-it-yourselfers under the Miles Home Ownership Plan.

If you are long on ambition but short on cash, you may have a friend at Miles Homes. The Miles Home Ownership Plan requires no down payment and only low monthly payments while you build. Miles puts its trust in people who are *capable* and *willing* to do all or most of the carpentry work involved in building a Miles home themselves.

For what is essentially a monthly finance charge, ranging from $150 to $270, Miles will deliver all materials needed to build one of its houses and give you three full years to complete it. Monthly payments do not begin until 60 days after the first delivery of materials. Once the house is completed, it becomes your responsibility to obtain permanent long-term financing from a local mortgage lender and pay off your debt to Miles.

Most of the more than 12,000 do-it-yourselfers who have built a Miles home took from six months to a year to complete their houses. With a house worth anywhere from 50 to 80 percent more than the cost of the components as collateral, few of them had any trouble obtaining a long-term mortgage once the structure was up. There is no pre-payment penalty for paying your Miles account in full at any time, and you only pay finance charges for the amount of time you owe Miles Homes money.

Miles homes are constructed piece by piece, from mostly pre-cut materials. Other than doors and windows, there are no prefabricated or panelized parts. Miles, however, makes many of the more difficult cuts before the materials are bundled for delivery to the customer. Still other components are carefully marked to show where pieces are joined.

No two Miles homes are alike. You have many choices of materials, outside and inside, and can even change the dimensions of the basic plan. The cost of the package is based on your specifications. While Miles does offer 34 basic plans, the company will also pre-cut the materials for any one of the thousands of plans sold by the plans catalog houses or a custom plan for something special you may have in mind.

There are no builder/dealers involved here. Nor does Miles expect customers to turn the project over to a contractor, though sub-contractors may be required for such things as electrical work and plumbing. You are expected to do as much of the work as you can. Step-by-step instructions are provided in a 104-page construction guide.

Materials are delivered to the site as they are needed, with framing and exterior materials delivered first. After the exterior is erected and weathertight, materials for the interior are delivered. The basic Miles home kit includes everything from sill plates and siding to coat hooks and 10 feet of kitchen cabinets. At extra cost, Miles will furnish paint, tile and some masonry materials, additional kitchen cabinets, heating, plumbing, and electrical supplies. Deliveries are made from plants located in Wilkes-Barre, Pennsylvania; Butler, Indiana; Atlanta, Georgia; Minneapolis, Minnesota; and Dallas, Texas. Miles serves all of the U.S. except the far-western states, Alaska, and Hawaii. It plans to extend operations to the West Coast in the near future.

The house shown is adapted from the basic Mt. Vernon, a two-story Colonial design with four bedrooms, plus attached garage. Under the Miles Home Ownership Plan, monthly payments for the basic Mt. Vernon kit would be $170 or less per month.

Most of the 50 plans in the Miles catalog are for ranch houses. There also are a few split-levels, split-foyers, and one-and-one-half-story designs. Living areas range from approximately 850 to 2,000 square feet and kit prices from $15,000 to $26,000.

It should be pointed out that Miles signs contracts on only about half of the orders its salesmen write. The success of the Miles financing program is directly related to its careful screening of applicants and the rejection of those who fail to convince Miles' managers of their ability and willingness to build a house without a good deal of expensive professional help.

**Miles' homes are constructed piece by piece, from mostly pre-cut materials. Other than doors and windows, there are no prefabbed or panelized parts.**

**The interior of the living-room wing added to the original plan reflects the attention to detail required of the successful owner-builder.**

**Willingness—or the patience—to do the work is a prerequisite if you expect to achieve results as professional as this.**

**floor plan of the Mt. Vernon**

**Miles' basic Mt. Vernon design**

COURTESY OF MILES HOMES, INC.; EXTERIOR AND INTERIOR PHOTOS BY BILL HEDRICH, HEDRICH-BLESSING

# Capp Homes/The Virginian

A colonial-styled house for the large family, the Virginian, by Capp Homes, is a Finish-It-Yourself house. Finish-It-Yourself means just that. Capp custom-builds the house on the lot and foundation you provide, but only through the enclosed shell stage. Under the plan, all materials needed to complete the house are included in the price.

Capp Homes is a pre-cut custom-home builder specializing in finish-it-yourself houses. Since 1946, over 50,000 families have built Capp homes, doing the finishing work themselves or hiring others to do some or all of it for them.

Whether built from the customer's plans, developed from a sketch or an idea, or a customized design from the Capp collection, Capp carpenters build the shell of the house on a foundation provided by the customer, according to the plan and Capp specifications. When the carpenters leave, the house is totally enclosed, with interior stud partitioning and sub-flooring installed, and doors and windows that lock.

The Capp Finish-It-Yourself package includes all the necessary finishing materials, from siding and sheetrock to plumbing and heating packages. Step-by-step guides show the owner how to finish his house, with complete instructions on the tools required and where to start.

Even if he chooses not to finish the entire house himself, he can be his own general contractor and still save, because he eliminates the middleman's profit. The more he does, the more he saves.

Most finishing jobs aren't all that difficult. Installing insulation in a Capp home, for instance, only requires the cutting of the insulation batt to size with a special knife and stapling it up. Other finishing jobs, like hanging doors, installing trim, or installing the kitchen cabinets, are no great challenge. Even installation of electric wiring can be learned quickly. Here, it's mostly leading wiring from outlets to switches and fixtures and then connecting the outlets to the service panel.

The Virginian, shown here, with approximately 1,650 square feet of floor space, is one of over 50 basic designs included in the Capp Planning Guide. It is a Colonial-styled home for the large family. Four bedrooms occupy the perimeter of the second floor. The master bedroom features its own bath and a closet with bypass doors. On the first floor, a full-width living room includes a suggested fireplace, and is separated from the large kitchen and dining area in the back. A half-bath is off the foyer, and a cozy den completes the first-floor layout.

Total Capp price for the Virginian is $35,495. This includes the erected shell, ready for finishing, complete with plumbing, heating, wiring, lighting fixtures, cabinets, appliances, floor tile, and carpeting ready for installation by the owner.

Other Capp designs include ranch, Spanish, and split-level models. Prices for Capp Finish-It-Yourself homes start at around $21,000 for a three-bedroom, 928-square-foot rustic ranch.

General marketing area for Capp Homes, which is a division of Evans Products Company, is from the Midwest to the Far West. Another Evans division, Ridge Homes, markets Finish-It-Yourself houses in the East.

floor plan of the Virginian

Capp carpenters install sub-flooring, interior stud-partitioning, and exterior doors and windows—so you wind up with a house that's enclosed and ready for you to finish.

the Virginian with a "ranch" exterior

# Cedar Forest Products/The Greenwood

More than 1,750 square feet of indoor space gives this three-bedroom Cedar Forest Products home a sense of spaciousness and lifetime luxury. It's an exciting home for the family with multiple interests.

Cedar Forest Products' pre-cuts feature single-wall construction, with all perimeter walls fitted together from 5 × 8-inch western red cedar timbers. The timber is actually a five-part laminate, factory bonded and kiln dried to provide high dimensional stability and full protection against moisture or leaks. No additional finish is required, inside or out.

Every CFP home is tailored to exact specifications, and all walls are pre-assembled at the factory to verify precision fit. Once the accuracy has been confirmed, the walls, with each timber coded to the re-construction plan, are dismantled, packaged with the other components, and shipped to the purchaser's building site.

Most of CFP's more than two dozen different pre-cuts can be built with nominal skills. Timbers are tongue-and-grooved and end-matched to mate perfectly. All electric outlets are pre-planned and timber courses are routed and/or drilled for Romex or other wiring. Starter holes are pre-drilled for 10-inch spikes at 5-foot intervals to speed wall construction. The customer is even offered a choice of corner styles: rustic "log-cabin" ends or "Salem square," either of which assembles easily and quickly. But CFP can provide whatever level of supervision may be needed, or complete contracting services.

The house shown here is the Greenwood, which has been designed to take advantage of a sloping site. More than 1,750 square feet of indoor floor space give this three-bedroom house a sense of spaciousness and lifetime luxury—with a 36-foot-long balcony serving the upper level, an 8 × 14-foot covered front porch, a 16 × 20-foot living room, and bathrooms on both levels. The large utility room could also serve as a workshop/toolroom. This is a practical house for the family with multiple interests.

Package price for the Greenwood is $25,928, F.O.B. Polo, Illinois. The package includes all building materials needed to complete the house, with the exception of the foundation and floor system. The floor system can be ordered as a packaged option at $3,740.

CFP offers western red cedar timber homes in a number of styles, including ranch, chalet, and split-level. Sizes range from a little over 500 to nearly 3,500 square feet.

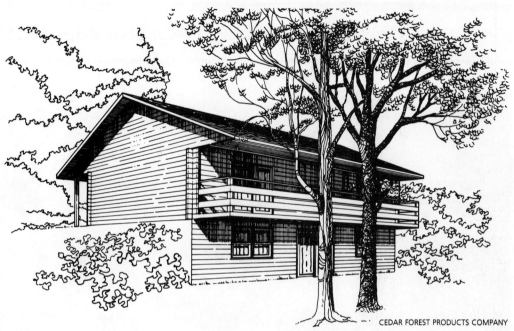

**another view of the Greenwood**

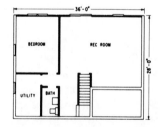

**floor plan of the Greenwood**

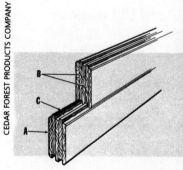

**details of glu-lam timbers used in CFP wall construction**

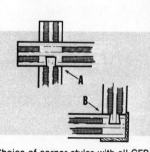

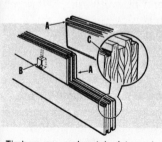

Nominal 5x8 western red cedar timbers used for all wall construction (A). New impervious five-part bonded laminate (B) provides full protection against moisture or leaks. Special form-filling adhesive (C) assures total seal between courses.

Choice of corner styles with all CFP buildings. Rustic "log cabin" ends (A) or "Salem square" (B). Either style completely sealed and impervious to wind and all weather; yet assemble easily and quickly.

Timbers are end-matched to mate perfectly for precision assembly (A). All electric outlets (B) are pre-planned to meet your needs. Timber courses are routed and/or drilled (C) for Romex or other wiring.

# Haida Hide/The Two-Story Gambrel

Haida Hide's Two-Story Gambrel takes a few liberties with traditional gambrel design, but it's an attractive and spacious dwelling with great versatility.

For the family that needs more space and yet is looking for something out of the ordinary, Haida Hide's Gambrel homes are an attractive and unique alternative. Based more or less on the traditional 1½-story Cape Ann Colonial, with a gambrel roof, central entrance, and downstairs bedroom, the Haida Hide Gambrels expand the design with dormers to provide full standing height along the outside walls, and outside cedar decks and balconies.

Haida Hide is recognized for the quality of its components and designs and has been shipping housing internationally for over a decade. It also gets high marks for energy conservation and now offers as standard, nationwide, what it used to call its Alaska package. This includes premium-grade red cedar siding, insulated glass doors and windows throughout, and an insulation value for exterior walls of R-14 and for roofs of R-20.

The Haida Hide Gambrel building system includes prefabricated exterior wall sections complete with studs, plates, and framed window openings. Frames for glass doors and the fireplace are also built into the system. The roof decking and interior vaulted ceiling are pre-cut tongue-and-groove hemlock with skylights available.

Engineered to close tolerances for quick and accurate assembly, the Gambrels are designed to fit any type of setting: level to steep lots in the city, suburban areas, or recreational land. Materials furnished with the basic Gambrel package include floor, wall, and roof systems, wall and roof insulation, doors, windows, stairway, interior partitioning, sheetrock (for interior walls and main floor ceiling), and all framing nails, finishing nails, flashing, and miscellaneous hardware required for erection of the package.

There are six different models in the Haida Hide Gambrel series. All measure 24 feet from front to rear. Widths go from 24 to 44 feet, with 4-foot increments. Dormer width increases in 2-foot increments, beginning at 6 feet for the 24 × 24-foot Gambrel. Floor areas range from 1,152 to 2,112 square feet, kit prices from $20,450 to $34,880, F.O.B. Seattle, Washington.

Haida Hide also has multi-model Chalet and Low-Profile homes series.

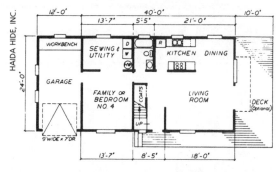

**MAIN FLOOR** **SECOND FLOOR**

floor plan of the Haida Hide Two-Story Gambrel

Prefabricated exterior-wall sections complete with studs, plates, and framed window openings are positioned prior to being secured to the deck to box-in the first level.

Dormer view walls and end-wall panels are positioned on the second-floor deck before being raised to support the roof girders.

Nestled on a wooded ridge, Acorn's Village House 1700-Special derives its unique design by the joining of a series of 12- and 16-foot sheds which, when cantilevered, maximize upper-level space and keep foundation costs to a minimum. Interesting forms are provided, inside and out.

Northern Homes' Point Breeze is pure modern design in every sense. The more trees that surround this house, the more dramatic the design becomes. A wide deck wraps around the living room on three sides, functionally as well as visually expanding the living space.

Featuring a symmetrically hipped roof capped with a large domed skylight, Acorn Structures' attractively simple Sky Dome I can be adapted for a two-level design or joined together with a second Sky Dome to double the living area. The square houses are particularly at home along sea or lake shores.

Reflecting the trend toward compact houses, the Pedestal home by Logangate Homes offers two bedrooms, two baths, living room, dining room, kitchen, and loft area—a comfortable environment for a small family—in 1,152 square feet of living space. In addition, the 16 x 16-foot basement/pedestal can be heated for use as a workshop and utility area. As a pre-cut and panelized kit, the Pedestal home costs approximately $15,000, plus options.

# CONTEMPORARIES

In the architect's lexicon, "contemporary" is probably best described as "functional modern"—which means it's not twenty-first-century modern. It's a cross between traditional and modern and owes much to Frank Lloyd Wright, the great American architect, and to the German Bauhaus school of Walter Gropius, which became famous in the 1920s for its experimental use of metal and glass in architecture.

Utilizing lots of glass and modern building materials, but eschewing ornamentation, the classic function of a contemporary design is to integrate the interior and the surrounding outdoor space. The interior arrangements usually are quite flexible and more open than those found in traditional houses. Decks, a common feature of contemporary design, act as natural extensions of the interior living space.

There are contemporaries that are adaptable to city and suburbia, but for the most part, contemporaries serve best for informal country living. They are very popular in newer vacation communities. Lest we work ourselves into a corner here, some builders use the term "contemporary" to cover almost any building style with clean, modern lines that is a departure from traditional ranch, Cape Cod, and two-story designs.

The newest look in contemporaries are asymmetrical houses that appear to have been created by clustering a number of wooden buildings, each rising to a different height and with individual, steeply pitched roofs. Proving there's nothing new under the sun, these actually come down from the old country houses of New England, which were often expanded by adding buildings with offsetting rooflines and shed-shaped wings, the roofs of which were pitched to discard heavy snows. The design also works well in the South and Southwest, where the multi-level roofs, with air spaces beneath them, can help dispel the heat of a relentless sun.

Most contemporary designs lend themselves to easy expansion to keep up with a growing family. The one thing that might turn you away is that only a few of the companies featuring contemporary designs gear their business toward the individual who wants to build his house from the ground up. You may have to settle for working with a builder/dealer and perhaps take over at some finishing stage of construction, with the shell completed and the mechanicals (wiring, plumbing, and heating systems) roughed in.

**The Deck House is a perfect blend of aesthetics and function, making liberal use of glass and decks that act as natural extensions of the interior living space. It would be difficult to find a Deck House that wasn't contemporary.**

**Special attention is given to the flow of space in a Deck House interior. Space expands horizontally through walls of glass out onto decks, and vertically to soaring ceilings.**

# Kingsberry Homes/The Tahoe II

The Tahoe II blends the natural warmth and beauty of redwood perfectly into a truly striking architectural design. More than a home that's easy to look at, it's a home that's genuinely easy to live in.

Boise Cascade, through its Manufactured Housing Division/Eastern Operations, is one of the nation's leading producers of panelized houses. With over 170 different models, selling for approximately $20,000 to $100,000 exclusive of land costs, the houses are marketed under the Kingsberry Homes brand name. They are distributed through more than 1,200 independent builders in 40 states east of the Rockies and from plants located in Alabama, Iowa, Oklahoma, Virginia, and Pennsylvania.

Representative of the many fine Kingsberry Homes, the Tahoe II, built for year-round or vacation living, combines the natural warmth and beauty of redwood lap siding with truly striking contemporary styling. Inside, from the high-ceilinged living room and dining areas, the well-planned kitchen and the two convenient downstairs bedrooms with bath to the secluded upstairs bedroom with its own bath and walk-in closet, it's no less appealing.

Completed by a Kingsberry Homes builder, and including appliances, plumbing fixtures, and floor covering, but excluding the cost of the land and site improvements, the 1,288-square-foot Tahoe II would cost from $32,000 to $45,000, depending on building costs in your area and the extras you order. If you arrange to do a substantial amount of the finishing work yourself, the cost could be brought down accordingly.

The buyer wishing to reduce the cost of his house with sweat equity would have to make arrangements with one of the builders handling Kingsberry Homes. He could not buy the package directly from Boise Cascade. A typical arrangement might be to have the builder leave the lower level of a tri-level, or the upper floor of a Colonial design, unfinished. Or, possibly, the owner *might* be able to take over once the house has been dried in, with walls, roof, doors, and windows installed, which, with a Kingsberry Home, takes no time at all.

As much of the construction as possible is done in the factory. The cutting of the lumber and the nailing of the various pieces that go into the homes is almost exactly the same as you would see in a house built stick by stick on a building site. However, using automatic nailing machines and other precision tools that leave no room for error, the workmanship is as good as, if not better than, the best found in on-site construction today. The more efficient utilization of raw materials and the substantially reduced needs for expensive on-site labor bring in a better house at lower costs.

Panels come from the factory framed and sheathed, with windows and insulation, and even much of the siding, already installed. The trucks that deliver the package are loaded so the prefabricated wall and floor panels can be used in the sequence they come off the truck. Using hoists and other mechanical aids, a Kingsberry crew needs only a few days to dry in a house on a foundation that's been previously prepared.

With Tudor, Spanish, French Provincial, Dutch Colonial, ranch style, California Modern, Garrison New England Colonial, plus other traditional designs, many contemporaries, and a selection of distinguished vacation homes, it's doubtful that many other manufacturers offer as great a variety of well-designed houses as does Kingsberry Homes.

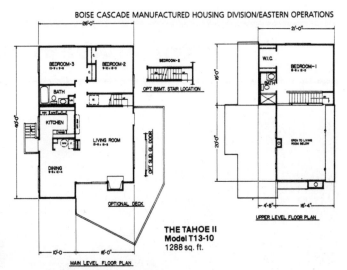

**floor plan of the Tahoe II**

**art showing another view of the Tahoe II**

# Acorn Structures/Village House 1400

An Acorn Village House is a group of shed shapes joined together in a pleasing way to make interesting exterior forms and to make effective use of interior spaces. Village House 1400 is a compact, three-bedroom plan.

The New England home, unique in its character and efficiency, is the basis of Acorn Structures' design approach. As demonstrated in its 30 standard models, Acorn's architects, using many tested design and construction elements from homes of an earlier day, have successfully blended the traditional and the contemporary. Typical Acorn touches are to isolate entryways from living areas and to locate fireplaces centrally for more efficient heating.

Acorn's 30 designs fall into five major groupings: Farm Houses, Shed Shapes, Country Houses, Square Houses, and Steep Roofs. The designs cover the full range, from small homes for small families or vacation use to large, multi-level structures with five bedrooms.

Shown here is one of Acorn's five Village Houses, which derive their name and distinct design from village-like clusters of 12- and 16-foot sheds. In the Village House series, all entries, kitchens, living and dining rooms, as well as master bedrooms, have cathedral ceilings. The houses, part of Acorn's Farm Houses group, lend themselves to additions, for more living space, or a variety of outbuildings.

Village House 1400 is a compact, yet spacious, single-level, three-bedroom plan. On a sloping site, the basement can provide additional living space. Or if the basement is eliminated, the stairwell becomes a laundry/utility room. As a ready-to-move-in, dealer-built house, with carpeting, fireplace, and kitchen installed, you'd pay between $50,000 and $60,000 for this house. But you also have the option to buy the house as an erected shell (weathertight structure on specified foundation, with studded partitions, stairs, and decks in place), or rough finished (erected shell with plumbing, heating, electrical service, insulation, and sheetrock installed) and finish it yourself. Price of the dealer-erected shell would fall somewhere between $30,000 and $40,000. Rough finish would be in the $40,000-to-$50,000 range.

Any of Acorn's builder/dealers, located mostly east of the Mississippi, can construct your home precisely as conceived. If you choose to build in a region that isn't served by an Acorn builder/dealer, an Acorn representative will work with you and the builder of your choice to assure a properly built Acorn home. Once ground is broken, it generally takes up to four months to complete most Acorns, less time if you elect rough finish and only a few weeks for an erected shell.

Panelized in 4-foot segments at Acorn's Acton, Massachusetts, factory, and using kiln-dried western lumber for greater strength and dimensional stability in framing and exterior walls, Acorn's system offers easy customizing or modification in design. Add four feet to the longest dimension of the Village House 1400 and the living room can be separated from the dining room by a dramatic fireplace, the kitchen from the family room by cabinets. Acorn encourages these and other touches that give a house its personality.

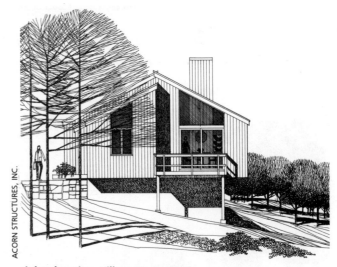

right elevation, Village House 1400

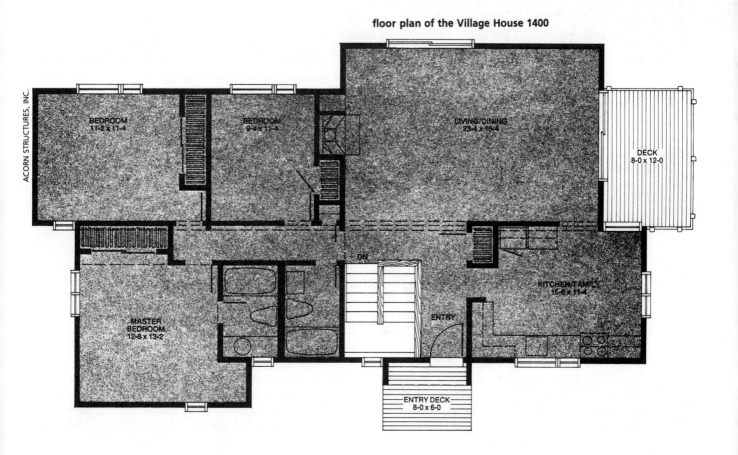

floor plan of the Village House 1400

# Pacific Frontier Homes/The Frontier VI

The Frontier home goes back to old-fashioned barn-building, with heavy exposed post-and-beam framing—a system that combines substance, simplicity, and rustic charm.

Although it wasn't part of Pacific Frontier Homes' original design concept, its building system, based on old-fashioned barn construction, with heavy, exposed-post-and-beam framing, has proven to be remarkably well adapted for the owner-builder. The system, which uses lots of redwood lumber, combines substance, simplicity, and rustic charm.

Once the pre-cut framing has been assembled, usually a two-day job for four men, 1½×6-inch tongue-and-groove redwood, which serves as the inside wall, is nailed horizontally to the outside face of the posts. Over this goes rigid urethane-foam insulation, waterproof felt paper, and then, vertically, on the outside, 1×8-inch rough-sawn tongue-and-groove redwood or western red cedar.

The roof system is equally rugged and includes 4-inch-thick Douglas fir rafters, 2-inch-tongue-and-groove pine decking, rigid foam insulation, and the finish roofing, either composition shingles or redwood shingles or shakes.

The construction is tolerant of minor errors, and the natural luxury of the redwood solves many decorating problems. Interior partitions can be either redwood posts and rough-sawn redwood paneling or conventional 2 × 4 framing with the finish of your choice.

Featured here is the contemporary-styled Frontier VI, which can be built in a number of sizes and floor plans. It is one of eight designs in the Frontier series. Also offered are chalets, "cottages," and starter houses that can easily be expanded. The standard Frontier VI, as shown, is a T-shaped, two-bedroom plan with 1,024 square feet of living area plus a 320-square-foot loft. It is an exceptional house for the owner contemplating a move out of the city into what may be a vacation home for a few years but will ultimately be a permanent home.

The Frontier package includes all lumber, connection hardware (except nails), exterior wood doors and redwood jambs, pre-glazed aluminum sash and patio doors, porch deck and joists, floor joists and sub-floor, finish roof, and wall, roof, and floor insulation. Price for the standard Frontier VI package is $22,880, F.O.B. Fort Bragg, California.

Pacific Frontier has shipped homes throughout the continental U.S. and to Hawaii. The company encourages the owner-builder to avail himself of the services of a factory representative for a day or two during the framing and has provided this service, for which there is a charge, as far away as Florida. When the representative leaves the job, after going over all aspects of the construction with the owner, he takes a set of job prints with him. It is rare that a problem arises that can't be handled over the phone with both the owner-builder and Pacific Frontier's representative looking at identical sets of plans.

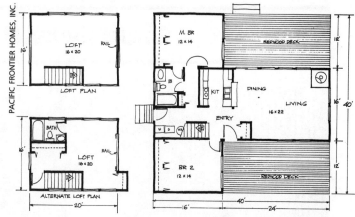

**floor plan of the Frontier VI**

**This is barn construction, simple and tolerant of minor errors. Modifications of the basic design are quite easy.**

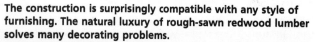

**The construction is surprisingly compatible with any style of furnishing. The natural luxury of rough-sawn redwood lumber solves many decorating problems.**

131

# Lindal Cedar Homes/The Nile

**floor plan of the Nile**

The tri-level Nile is a pleasing, practical design that uses space efficiently and lends itself to a "zoning" of activities.

There are a number of houses in this book that obviously, and sometimes not so obviously, are beyond the capabilities of inexperienced builders. Unless you are a thoroughly experienced craftsman with a lot of time at your disposal, construction of this house, at least through the shell stage, even though it comes as a completely pre-cut and parts-numbered package, is best left to a professional crew. With three levels and 2,280 square feet of floor space, it's just too much house for the amateur to tackle without a lot of experienced outside help.

The house is the Nile, and it's from Lindal Cedar Homes' River Series, which includes the even larger, 2,413-square-foot Amazon. As mentioned, the Nile is a tri-level—a pleasing, practical design that uses space efficiently and lends itself to the "zoning" of activities. It features four bedrooms and three baths. The entry level includes the living and dining areas, which are open to a cathedral ceiling. From the stairway, it's just a few steps down to the family room. Upstairs, the bedroom level is a third zone. The upstairs also enjoys the drama of high, peaked ceilings and open beams. A view into the living room below, over an open rail on the stairwell, adds an extra dimension of spaciousness.

Construction is post-and-beam, and the exterior wood is kiln-dried western red cedar. Price for the basic Nile package, F.O.B. New York or Atlanta, is $46,191. It could also be ordered from the factory in Tacoma, Washington. The basic package does not include inside doors, roof and wall insulation, interior wall and roof liner, the deck, garage, or foundation materials.

Lindal makes it easy for the prospective purchaser to explore the Nile—or any other specific Lindal plan—in detail, with a Plans Package consisting of three sets of construction plans, an illustrated construction manual, and a parts list. The package, which costs $50, enables the buyer and/or his builder to establish a preliminary construction schedule, cost out various sub-contract labor and materials, arrange financing, if appropriate, and even determine carpeting, drapery, and furniture needs. The cost of the Plans Package is deductible from the purchase price of the house.

There are 15 other Lindal design series and a total of 48 standard models. Kit prices run from about $17,370 for the 726-square-foot Bikini in the View Series, to $43,375 for the 2,789-square-foot Lincoln in the Presidential Series. Those are Basic package prices. Lindal also has Plus and Custom packages, which include such things as inside doors, insulation, and cedar shingles or shakes, rather than the brown-tone asphalt shingles included in the Basic package. The company is very active throughout North America, with over 150 independent distributors.

# Vacation Land Homes/The Mountain Haus

A new concept in housing introduced by Vacation Land Homes employs the modular philosophy but frees it from standardization. The basic Vacation Land modular-home package consists of from two to four rectangular units that may be assembled in a variety of configurations to suit the personal preferences and requirements of the owner. The modules, which come in half a dozen sizes, ranging from 12 × 24 to 14 × 40 feet, can be joined together all on the same level or stacked to provide bi-level living in keeping with the natural surroundings. Exteriors are rough-sawn cedar for minimum maintenance.

The handyman with a flair for carpentry may purchase these units in almost any unfinished state. This, in effect, provides prospective home owners with a starter package with which to complete the modular Vacation Land structure or serve as the nucleus for a custom-built house of the owner's own design variation.

A complete package can also be ordered, with Vacation Land responsible for everything from construction of the foundation to the electrical installation. The modules are constructed in Vacation Land's plant and are delivered to the customer's site by Vacation Land trucks and erection crews. Decorative features, roof lines, and floor plans can be altered while the order is being processed to make the house truly unique.

The Mountain Haus, shown here, is one of eight houses in Vacation Land's modular series, but the design possibilities are virtually limitless. Using four 14×24-foot modules, the three-bedroom, two-bath Mountain Haus includes over 1,350 square feet of living space, plus three decks. Base price for the shell package, which includes everything but the wood floors, is $25,161, F.O.B. Bellaire, Michigan.

Turn-key prices on Vacation Land's modular combinations, including carpeting, appliances, plumbing, heating, insulation, etc., range from $35,000 to $55,000. Vacation Land modulars usually take from 45 to 60 days to complete, once delivered to the building site.

**floor plan of the Mountain Haus**

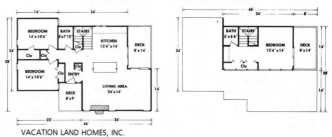

VACATION LAND HOMES, INC.

# Pre-Cut Timber Homes/The Belaire

One of four designs in Pre-Cut Timber Homes' Contemporary series, the Belaire features a master bedroom and bath on the upper level, two bedrooms on the lower level. The house is built log-cabin style, with glu-lam timbers offered in three thicknesses.

A Pre-Cut Timber Home is put together a lot like a log house, one course at a time around the entire perimeter, with little or no vertical framing. The "logs" with which the outer walls and interior support walls are assembled, however, are man-made rather than nature's own. Pre-Cut Timber "makes it better" by glue-laminating three or more thicknesses of kiln-dried western red cedar under intense heat and pressure. The result is a precisely manufactured structural member that interlocks to form a dimensionally stable, virtually indestructible wall, pre-finished inside and out.

Keystone of this single-wall-construction system is a patented tongue-and-groove "T" joint. All wall components are precision milled and are welded together with adhesive, without tapes or chinking. With the timbers offered in three thicknesses—nominal 3-inch, super 3-inch, and nominal 5-inch, the latter with double tongue-and-grooving—the walls have an insulating value of up to R-24, for a heat-loss factor less than half that of conventional framed buildings. The average Pre-Cut Timber home utilizes approximately 15,000 board feet of lumber, as compared to only 6,000 board feet in conventional construction.

In addition to the wall system, the Pre-Cut Timber package includes floor beams; sub-flooring; 2×6-inch tongue-and-groove decking and particle board overlayment for loft floors; the roof system, including insulation and shingles or shakes; windows, exterior and interior doors; and all nails, adhesive, and flashings needed to complete the house.

There are 42 home designs in Pre-Cut Timber's six design series. The three-bedroom Belaire, featured here, is one of four designs in the Contemporary series. (Other series are Alpine, Country, Leisure, Traditional, and

Western.) With the second-floor master bedroom and bath, the floor area of the Belaire totals 1,338 square feet.

Pre-Cut Timber homes are offered in Economy, Standard, and Deluxe packages. The principal difference is the thickness of the wall components. With nominal 3-inch walls, the kit price for the Belaire is $31,753, F.O.B. Woodinville, Washington.

Pre-Cut Timber can start you off on any type of program, from a total do-it-yourself package to a complete turn-key construction contract. Design services are $150 for stock plans and $250 for custom plans. These charges can be applied to the cost of the house.

More than half of Pre-Cut Timber's customers participate in the construction of their new home. Pre-Cut Timber houses can be found all the way from Alaska to New England. They adapt to any standard foundation system, including basement, post and piers, perimeter, or cantilevered.

**drawing of the Belaire**

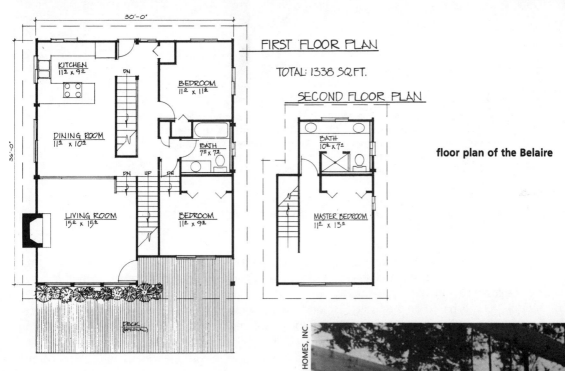

**floor plan of the Belaire**

**Keystone of American Timber's single-wall construction system is a patented tongue-and-groove joint. All wall components are precision-milled and are welded together with adhesive, without tapes or spikes.**

135

# Deck House/Model 7133

A typical Deck House design, the Model 7133, based on the basic Series 3 design for houses of less than 1,700 square feet, features an open living/dining room with views in three directions. Shaded by the carport, the recessed center entry to the house is a split design, with access to both the upper and lower levels.

There are as many Deck House plans as there are owners. The Deck House concept is based on a series of designs in a wide range of sizes—from under 1,700 to more than 3,500 square feet. These are the "starting points" for most of the Deck Houses being built today. This systems approach permits modifications and re-arrangements of existing designs at reasonable costs. The house featured here, Model 7133, is based on the basic Series 3 design, for houses of less than 1,700 square feet, with the attached carport created by extending the roof to shelter two cars at the entry level.

Deck Houses utilize post-and-beam construction, permitting an almost unlimited flexibility in a unique, solid structure. The pre-cut and shaped roof and floor beams (select structural 4 × 12 or 4 × 14 Douglas fir) are supported at the centerline and outside walls by concrete-filled steel columns and select structural 4 × 4 fir posts. It is this sturdy, rugged framing that supports the entire structure. Interior partitions are non-load bearing, permitting flexibility in room arrangement, as well.

Quality materials, precision engineering, generous roof overhangs, walls of glass, and the use of visually appealing cedar decking for the floors and as part of the roof system (with the exposed surface of inland red cedar creating a handsome ceiling throughout the house) are clear tipoffs to a Deck House.

The decking is Potlatch Lock-Deck, consisting of three kiln-dried boards laminated together with the center piece offset to give each plank a tongue and groove. The ends of the decking are also offset to ensure a tight fit on all four sides and to provide for easy on-site installation.

Deck House's marketing area is the continental U.S., but it does not have a builder/dealer setup. The company prefers to deal directly with the customer, many of whom take advantage of Deck House's orientation program at its headquarters in Acton, Massachusetts. There, the Manager of Builder Services goes over the particular working drawings, reviews pertinent details, and answers questions. This is supplemented with a slide presentation covering the construction aspects and a visit to several Deck Houses under construction in the area. This man remains only a phone call away in the event other questions arise during construction. There also are model houses that can be inspected in half a dozen states.

The component package, excluding the attached carport, for the 1,680-square-foot, split-entry Deck House presented here costs $25,000. If you don't do any of the work yourself, Deck House estimates you'd pay an additional $29,000 to have the house built by a local contractor. That price would include everything from the foundation to the mechanical systems and appliances. It comes out to $32 per square foot. While that cost is on a par with conventional construction, the materials, for the most part, are of a quality and finish detail found only in the finest custom-built houses.

With sub-assemblies and the factory preparation of other materials used to construct the shell of the house, most Deck Houses are weathertight within two weeks of the time erection begins.

**Deck House utilizes post-and-beam construction, permitting an almost unlimited flexibility in a unique, solid structure.**

**floor plan of the Deck House Model 7133**

Upper Level

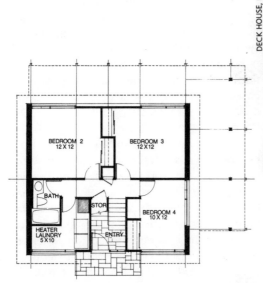

Lower Level

**In a Deck House, there always are spacious, light-washed areas for socializing with family and friends.**

137

# Pease/The Sequoia

From the two-story foyer to the family room off the kitchen, the Sequoia is a marvel of well-zoned space. But then Pease is noted for the interior planning as well as exterior detailing of its architect-designed houses.

Typifying the excellent quality that Pease Company provides in its houses, the Sequoia, with 2,514 square feet of living area, not including the garage, is a marvel of well-zoned space. From the two-story foyer, climb open-tread stairs to the "quiet level," where you will discover three bedrooms and a bonus room. Note the balcony overlooking the foyer in bedroom two. The cathedral ceiling is beamed in the living room-dining room areas, which are separated by a specially designed divider. The master bedroom has distinctive double doors just off the foyer.

Pease is noted for the exterior detailing and interior planning of its architect-designed houses. The company currently offers 44 contemporary and traditional ranch, bi-level, tri-level, and two-story models designed to structural standards that meet or exceed FHA specifications. Sizes range from the 1,248-square-foot Brunswick ranch to the 5,012-square-foot, two-story Promontory, the master suite of which utilizes 700 square feet, including bedroom, sitting area with wood-burning fireplace, two walk-in closets, a large dressing area, and a full bath, all with cathedral ceilings.

Pease goes beyond most packagers in that it not only provides the structural components, but also the materials used on the exterior and the interior of the structural system. Since 1893, Pease has been a reliable supplier of building products. A wide selection of items, ranging from exterior doors and hardboard sidings to kitchen cabinets and bathroom accessories, is carried by Pease and conveniently catalogued in the 152-page Pease Pricer.

Whether you choose to build a Pease house yourself, be your own general contractor, or have a contractor build it for you, you may include most anything shown in the Pease Pricer as an option in your home package. Each order is priced individually to facilitate this freedom of choice. The package includes not only all essential shell components, but interior partitions, doors, and trim. Base price for the Sequoia package is about $23,000, F.O.B. Hamilton, Ohio.

**floor plan of the Sequoia**

There's simple elegance in the foyer of the Sequoia. Note the bedroom balcony overlooking the foyer. That's the master bedroom at lower right.

PACIFIC FRONTIER HOMES, INC.

You can start small with the Frontier I-I, a 312-square-foot efficiency weekender by Pacific Frontier Homes, then add bedrooms and other features as needed. The tidy house can be expanded to a three-bedroom, two-bath Frontier I-3 at any time.

GREEN MOUNTAIN HOMES

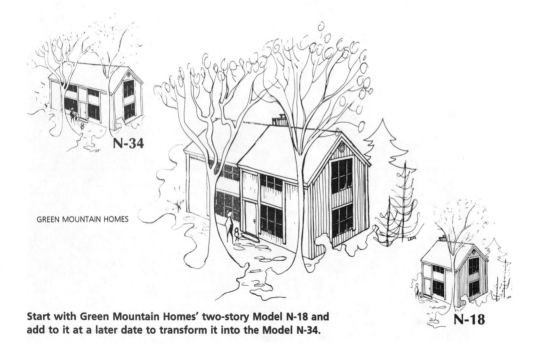

Start with Green Mountain Homes' two-story Model N-18 and add to it at a later date to transform it into the Model N-34.

# HIDEAWAYS & STARTERS

A house no bigger than a two-car garage might not be your idea of a dream house. It could, however, be your answer to home-ownership, or second-home-ownership. Good things *do* come in small packages, and there are any number of intriguing pre-cuts and pre-fabs that tuck everything into less than 400 square feet of living space. Included are wee houses that are designed to be expanded to keep up with a growing family, weekend hideaways that could be enlarged for retirement living later, and camps and cabins that a handyman can erect in locations accessible only by four-wheel-drive or snowmobile.

You can't build these economical compacts in a suburban subdivision zoned for $60,000 homes. But if you have land in the mountains, at the shore, or out in the country, and can swing the financing for a project budgeted at between $5,000 and $10,000, say, you can have a house today that includes all the essentials in an efficiency or weekender that can be expanded as needed or as your income allows. Many are perfectly designed to take advantage of economical wood stoves as a primary source of heat. And any house that is easy to heat will obviously be easy to cool. A spacious deck could double as the living area in good weather.

Bigger isn't always better, especially if you hope to conserve energy. Many single people and young couples who don't plan to have children are purposely building money-saving smaller houses today, both primary and vacation homes, with no intention of expanding them. However, if you do anticipate adding a bedroom, a living/dining room, or whatever, someday, plan the complete house at the outset. Complex areas such as the kitchen and the first bathroom should be in their positions on your final plan from the beginning. It would be difficult to relocate them at a later date.

Not all designs lend themselves to expansion. There are some log cabins in this category. While they make fine hunting camps and one- and two-bedroom retreats, the smaller units don't always shape up into retirement residences. Among the easiest structures to expand are domes and polygons. You simply add another unit, of whatever size, and connect the two.

**Measuring only 10 x 16 feet, Real Log Homes' Cabot is in the camp or cabin category. Ideal for those spots inaccessible to larger trucks, the pre-cut logs and other pieces could be delivered to the chosen site by a 4 x 4 pickup or even a snowmobile.**

**Bigger isn't always better, and a wee cabin like Building Logs' 16 x 22-foot Tincup could give you everything you'll ever want in a weekend hideaway.**

# Shelter-Kit/Unit One

**Designed for amateur builders, the expandable Unit One makes it easy to start building without a major financial investment.**

Shelter-Kit's well-engineered Unit One, a weathertight 12×12-foot modular shell with a shed roof, can be assembled in about four days by two unskilled builders. It has as options a 9×12-foot deck and a 9×12-foot roofed platform that can be enclosed to make an additional room. You can add any number of modules to build a larger house.

The Unit One with a deck, designed for use as a vacation cabin, ski lodge, guest house, or the start of a year-round home, is the simplest form of this modular house. A typical expansion would include converting the deck to a porch and adding another Unit One with an enclosed porch to make additional rooms. The modular system is designed to make such additions easy and practical. These structures can even be taken down and put up elsewhere.

All the materials needed to construct a Unit One shell are contained in the basic kit: pre-cut and pre-drilled quality lumber for the post-and-beam frame; screened sliding-glass doors and windows; flooring; siding; and roofing. The materials are labeled and bound together in bundles weighing approximately 100 pounds. All required hardware, from steel bolts to galvanized-steel joist connectors, is labeled and packed in separate containers.

The lumber bundles are light enough to be carried by two men to sites that can't be reached by a truck-and-trailer, so an approach road is not essential. Nor are power tools, since most of the components are bolted or nailed together. All tools required for assembly are furnished, including two 6-foot stepladders and two carpenters' aprons.

**floor plan for Kit #38**

**KIT 38**
1 Unit One
1 Porch
1 12' sliding glass door
1 5'x3' sliding window
1 set tools
Construction manual

142

Illustrated site-preparation and construction manuals make the assembly easy. The purchaser of a Unit One receives his manuals in advance of delivery of the kit, so he can have ample opportunity to become familiar with the construction procedures. Step-by-step instructions guide the builder to the completion of his house.

The post-and-beam frame, with its custom-designed heavy aluminum angles, makes it possible for the entire weight of both floor and roof to be carried by six posts. Thus, the walls are non-load-bearing and conventional structural bracing can be eliminated. This allows for sliding-glass doors across the entire front opening, and the placement of other doors and windows in virtually any location. Non-structural bracing is used to support the siding. When two or more Unit Ones are joined, the common walls can be eliminated.

Minimal disturbance to the environment is achieved by the simplicity of the foundation. The frame of the Unit One requires only a 10-inch-diameter poured-concrete pier for each of the six posts. Site-preparation instructions explain in detail where those piers are to be located and how they are formed.

The kits are shipped from the factory in Tilton, New Hampshire. Shelter-Kit has found that the most economical and convenient method of delivery is for them to rent a 16-foot U-Haul truck (or its equivalent) in the customer's name, load it, and then turn it over to the customer at the factory and let him drive it to the site. (The truck can later be turned in to the nearest U-Haul agency.) Two or three Unit Ones with deck or porch kits could be loaded in one truck.

Prices start at $2,682 for a Unit One kit and go to $12,881 for a three-bedroom plan that combines six Unit Ones and two decks for 1,171 square feet of living area. The units shown here are Cabin A (Kit 38—a Unit One with porch), priced at $3,296, and a one-bedroom plan (Kit 43—two Unit Ones, one deck, one enclosed porch), priced at $6,069.

**floor plan for Kit #43**

A Unit One can be assembled in about four days by two unskilled builders. The kit contains everything needed to complete the shell—pre-cut, pre-drilled lumber for the post-and-beam frame; screened sliding-glass doors and windows; flooring; siding; and roofing.

Shelter-Kit's one-bedroom plan (Kit #43, with 450 square feet) is made up from four modules: two Unit Ones, one enclosed porch, and one deck.

The walls of a Unit One are non-load-bearing, and common walls can be eliminated when two or more Unit Ones are joined, as in this cozy nest designed for year-round living.

143

# Timberpeg/Cluster Sheds

Three Cluster Shed buildings combine to create a delightful home which wraps around a secluded deck-terrace. Sliding patio doors can be placed in any of the full-height front bays to capture both sun and views.

Designed to be used individually or combined for expanded living space, Timberpeg's Cluster Sheds are another way to get started on that vacation home (or even full-time home) you were planning before building costs soared out of sight. With four basic Cluster Shed structures, ranging in floor area from 192 to 512 square feet, you can create exactly what you need and can afford at any given time—from a one-room weekend hideaway or starter unit to a multi-bedroom complex.

As your own architect and contractor, you can butt two or more Cluster Sheds together or link them with enclosed connectors, extend the length of any Unit, add a shed entry, solve the problem of a steep slope or otherwise difficult terrain by placing units on varying levels.

There's more to a Cluster Shed than meets the eye. The framing is solid 6 × 6 timbers; roof rafters are 4 × 6's. With pegged mortised-and-tenoned joints, there's no need for nails or spikes in assembling the frame. Beyond the structural integrity, the rugged, exposed post-and-beam construction permits unlimited interior arrangements. Much pleasure comes from living with the texture and beauty of natural wood.

A 12×16-foot Cluster Shed can be completed in a week. Built on a slab, piers, or over a partial or full basement, it's a fine vacation project that will provide lasting value and satisfaction. Once the frame and rafters are in place, one person can finish the job by himself. Wall and roof construction is the same as with the larger Timberpeg houses (see page 112). Fully detailed plans and a step-by-step construction guide are provided.

The pre-cut Cluster Shed kit includes the post-and-beam framing timbers and roof rafters, all precisely mortised or tenoned; oak pegs; all necessary lumber for interior and exterior walls; rigid insulation for walls and roof; hand-split cedar shakes; windows and wood-framed patio doors with tempered, insulating glass.

Kit prices: Cluster Shed #1, 12 × 16 feet, $4,093; Cluster Shed #2, 12 × 32 feet, $8,186; Cluster Shed #3, 16 × 24 feet, $8,062; Cluster Shed #4, 16 × 32 feet, $10,746. All prices are F.O.B. Claremont, New Hampshire.

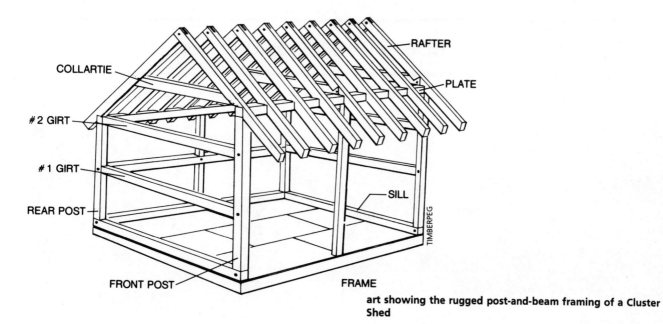

art showing the rugged post-and-beam framing of a Cluster Shed

A Cluster Shed #2 building coupled with a #3 building. The connecting link houses a full bath and an entry with closet and utility space.

### the Cluster Shed series

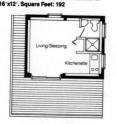

Cluster Shed #1. Overall Dimensions: 16'x12'. Square Feet: 192

Cluster Shed #2. Overall Dimensions: 32'x12'. Square Feet: 384

Cluster Shed Design #32. Overall Dimensions: 51'x32'. Square Feet: 933

Cluster Shed #3. Overall Dimensions: 24'x16'. Square Feet: 384

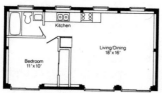

Cluster Shed #4. Overall Dimensions: 32'x16'. Square Feet: 512

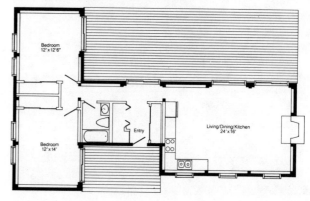

# Pre-Cut Timber Homes/Leisure Series

Pre-Cut Timber Homes' Bunkhouse totals only 192 square feet, including 75 square feet of screened porch. Here, the snug Bunkhouse serves as a satellite bedroom to the larger Islander, at left.

Engineered for easy future expansion, Pre-Cut Timber Homes' Leisure Series includes a number of noteworthy one- and two-bedroom designs that can help beat the high cost of acquiring a vacation home and/or getting an early start on providing for retirement living. The 272-square-foot Maui, the 400-square-foot Laguna, the 484-square-foot Sawdust, and the 506-square-foot Rendezvous could win a slew of converts to the philosophy that small is beautiful.

If you really want to start small, you could build Pre-Cut Timber's Bunkhouse, which, including 75 square feet of screened porch, totals only 192 square feet. The snug Bunkhouse, as shown, actually serves as a satellite to the Islander, a considerably larger house measuring 23 × 36 feet.

Unlike most vacation "cottages," Pre-Cut Timber's western red cedar homes are built to meet or exceed FHA, as well as virtually all local and state, code requirements for primary homes. Built log-cabin style, with little or no framing, the walls of a Pre-Cut Timber leisure home are assembled one level at a time, around the entire perimeter, with interlocking laminated structural members that are three inches thick.

This is tongue-and-groove, single-wall construction—with a finished inside and outside wall and insulation all in one. All joints are welded with an adhesive for a weathertight seal. Thanks to the natural insulation value of the solid wood walls, the houses are easy to heat and cool and can be adapted for year-round living.

Pre-Cut Timber kits include wall, floor, and roof system materials, windows, exterior and interior doors, inside and outside trim, and all necessary nails, adhesive, and flashings. Leisure Series prices begin at $7,348, for the Maui, F.O.B. Woodinville, Washington.

There are eight models in all in Pre-Cut Timber's energy-efficient Leisure Series. The company also offers larger vacation and primary homes in alpine, contemporary (see page 134), country, traditional, and western styling.

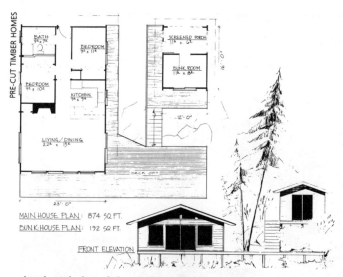

**sketch and plan of the Islander Bunkhouse**

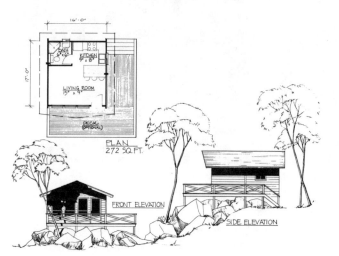

**sketch and plan of the Maui**

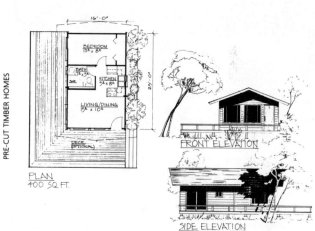

**sketch and plan of the Laguna**

**sketch and plan of the Sawdust**

**sketch and plan of the Rendezvous**

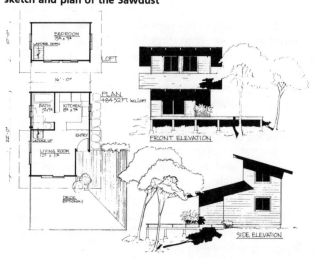

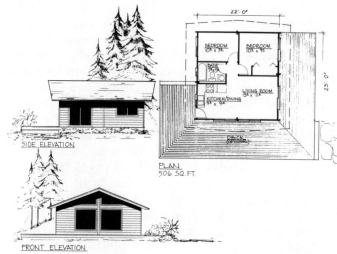

147

# SOLAR HOUSES

The innovative, energy-saving houses of Green Mountain Homes combine passive solar design with the classic barn shapes of the New England countryside.

You can't just tack a solar system onto a house and expect big energy savings. Unless the house is designed to be energy efficient, a solar system, even with a substantial tax write-off, can be a poor investment. There are priorities to be met here, and anyone building a house today would be foolish not to observe such energy-saving fundamentals as orientation of the house to benefit from natural solar gain, and adequate insulation to keep winter heat in, summer heat out.

Site orientation is critical not only for energy efficiency, but also for the placement of solar collectors. Where winters are cold and the north wind strong, the optimum compass orientation for major glass areas is a little west of south. Through the winter months, the sun rises and sets well to the south of the east/west line, and the north side of the house receives little or no sunshine. The fewer windows on that side, the better. A 3×5-foot, north-facing window can lose as much as 15,000 BTU's on a frigid day. That same expanse facing south can produce a gain of 9,500 BTU's. That's a swing of 24,500 BTU's—or 7 KWH if you plan to use conventional electric resistance heat; a quart of oil with an oil-fired furnace.

Passive solar systems are based on this potential heat gain through large, south-facing windows. When sunlight passes through glass, it is transformed into heat energy. This is the "greenhouse effect," and often it can accomplish the same ends as active solar systems, which, with all their external hardware, may spoil the look of what you want in a house.

A built-in solar system includes not only a large amount of strategically placed glass, but an interior design that allows air to circulate freely and entryways that minimize the influx of cold air whenever an outside door is opened. With passive solar design, bedrooms usually are placed to the north, and family living areas to the south, to take maximum advantage of the sunlight.

As the sun climbs toward the summer solstice, south-facing windows receive less than half the winter insolation. But all that glass *can* raise summertime temperatures and cause the air conditioner to work overtime. It's good planning to shade south-facing windows with generous overhangs that won't impair heat gain in winter. In preventing unwanted heat gain, overhangs are much more effective than drapes, blinds, or shades inside the house.

The most important insulation in any house is at the top. Without adequate insulation, it's here that you'll have your greatest heat losses in the winter, heat gains in the summer. With older houses, insulation was simply laid in the floor of the attic. But fewer designs include an attic today, and insulation has become part of the roof system. Increasingly, it is being sandwiched between the roof decking or sheathing and the finish roofing. You still have the option of stapling batts of Fiberglas to the underside of the roof, between the rafters, but where roof decking serves as the ceiling, which is common with A-frames, chalets, and post-and-beam construction, a high-density, rigid-foam type of insulation is installed above the decking.

How much insulation is enough? It depends on the climate, of course. But Deck House has found that the optimum level for roof insulation (at least in the Boston area) is two inches of very efficient insulation board. A study published by the Forest Service, U.S. Department of Agriculture, agrees that after the R value (the material's ability to resist the passage of heat) exceeds 22 with a closed-cell-based insulation, you've reached the point where *extra* insulation does not make enough difference to justify the cost. FHA's minimum standard for roof insulation calls for a value of R-11.

With in-the-wall insulation, it's not so much the thickness of the insulation (the FHA minimum is R-7) as how methodically and precisely it is placed to seal all crevices around doors and windows. Here, as a kit-builder, you've got an edge. With precision pre-cut parts, panelized construction, pre-hung and insulated doors and windows, most kit-built houses are significantly more energy-efficient than conventional stick-built houses. And with log and dome homes, there are further gains. As pointed out earlier, log and dome construction can contribute to energy savings of up to 50 percent over conventional FHA stud-wall construction. There are other benefits here. Tight construction not only lowers fuel bills, but the initial cost of heating and cooling equipment, since capacities need not be as great. A tightly built house is also essential with electric resistance heating.

A word about windows. There's not much you can do to reduce heat loss through windows without investing in thermal curtains and the like. The R value of double-sealed windows—two panes and dead air space between—is only 1.65, and triple sealed, R-2.13. For most areas, including the South, where the main energy focus is on cooling, there would be little reason to go beyond double-sealed windows.

Active solar systems as opposed to passive solar systems include an array of roof-mounted collectors to gather solar energy. The heat gain is transferred via mechanically circulated air or liquid to a storage facility in the basement and drawn on as needed, again through heat transfer, by conventional domestic-hot-water and space-heating systems.

At least one system stores solar heat in tons of small stones inside an A-frame-shaped collector installed in the yard. But with other systems, a basement storage area almost always is essential, either for a heat-storing rock pile, or a large, heat-storing water tank. Also essential is a large, southern roof exposure at a pitch that takes maximum advantage of the sun's radiant energy through the winter months.

Don't look for a system that will satisfy all your heating needs. It should be considered a supplement to, rather than a substitute for, conventional heating systems. In most areas of the country, the storage capacities—and costs—won't justify a solar system that supplies more than 50 to 70 percent of the total heat needed. As it is, a solar system will add at least 10 percent to the cost of the house. Solar space-heating systems cost $8,000 and up just for the hardware. You've also got to figure on a basement, which you might not have been planning, and the costs of that steep roof, which takes more material to build and at higher labor costs than a conventional roof.

As far as solar air conditioning and photovoltaic electric systems go, they're still in the developmental stages and prohibitively expensive. Maybe they'll be something to think about when your pre-schooler grows up and builds *his* house.

In addition to the kit manufacturers represented with solar houses in the next pages, several dome manufacturers, including Monterey Domes and The Big Outdoors People, and at least one log house manufacturer, Lodge Logs by MacGregor, have introduced solar houses or systems designed for specific models.

# Solartran/The Galaxy

The Galaxy combines sleek contemporary styling with a super-efficient floor plan to offer convenient and exciting living with all sorts of special bonuses. A functional greenhouse is an integral part of this spacious family home.

Solartran Corporation offers four different, pre-packaged solar houses. Two of the houses incorporate a total solar design concept. The other two are traditionally styled houses designed to be energy-efficient and to which appropriate solar-heating equipment can be added. Solartran offers both circulating-air and liquid-type heat-collecting systems. Utilizing heat exchangers and hooked up to conventional domestic-hot-water and warm-air space-heating systems, they can substantially reduce monthly energy costs. The basic house packages are prepared for Solartran by American Timber Homes.

Shown here is the Galaxy, a spacious three-bedroom house designed for Solartran by Donald Watson, a well-known solar architect and the author of three books on solar heating. The Galaxy's large expanses of south-facing glass make an important contribution in passive solar heating. A functional greenhouse is an integral part of the house, the interior design of which includes a cathedral ceiling in the greenhouse and sun room areas.

On the north side, the location of the garage serves as a buffer to the north wind. Provision is made for a full basement, offering space not only for the storage of solar heat, but for a recreation room and additional closets.

The basic package of pre-cut and panelized parts includes 2 × 6 studs (sized to accommodate a wider variety of insulating materials), sheathing and felt, rough-sawn tongue-and-groove cedar siding, timber trusses, 2-inch-tongue-and-groove roof decking, joists and the upper-level sub-floor, interior pine paneling, partitioning, the stair system, triple-glazed windows, and pre-hung doors. Materials for the attached double garage also are included.

The owner is responsible for the foundation and first-floor deck, which should be in place before the Solartran package arrives. Shingles and roofing felt, insulation, drywall, and finish flooring are all purchased locally by the owner or his builder.

Price for the Galaxy package is about $45,000, which

includes delivery to job sites accessible by semi-trailer truck in most states east of the Mississippi and as far as Colorado to the west. A liquid-type solar-heat-collecting system for the Galaxy costs approximately $8,000 and includes 16 flat-plate collectors, circulating pump and control system, domestic-hot-water tank, heat exchangers, blower, damper, and heat-transfer liquid.

An optional high-efficiency wood-burning fireplace, which utilizes a water-heat-exchanger in the firebox and uses outside air for combustion, can be coupled with the solar system. When the fireplace is in use, a thermostat automatically turns on a water pump and circulates water through the heat-exchanger coil. The heated water is sent via pump to the main storage tank. Price of the fireplace package, including heat exchanger, capacitor, pump, valves, thermostat, expansion and reservoir tank, together with fireplace screen, heat-resistant glass door, flue pipe, and combustion air intake, is approximately $900.

The completed cost of the 1,847-square-foot Galaxy, if built by a contractor, could run to $90,000 and up, not including land, sewer, water, and site improvements. Solartran's least expensive solar house is the 1,050-square-foot, two-bedroom Sun Wedge. That one could be brought in for about half the cost of the Galaxy.

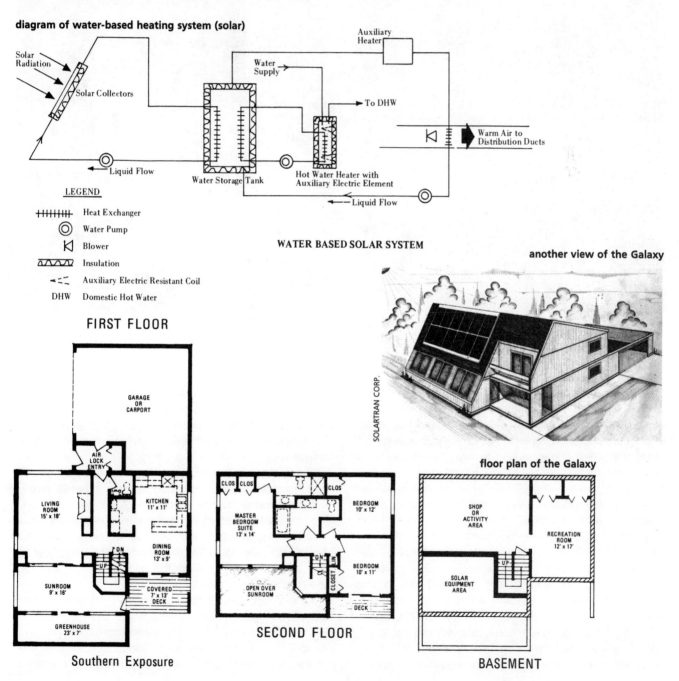

# Green Mountain Homes/N-38 Solar Home

view of the N-38 Solar Home

Green Mountain homes combine the classic barn shapes of the New England countryside with passive solar design that eschews the usual roof-mounted collectors and other hardware and provides an average of 37 percent of the energy needed to heat the house. This solar contribution is based on actual measurements during the winter of 1976–77 at a model home in Royalton, Vermont. It should be higher in areas with less severe weather conditions.

These innovative, energy-saving houses use east-, west-, and south-facing windows to collect heat via the greenhouse effect. The entire house is a solar collector and storage unit. Excess heat is stored within the first-floor concrete sub-system—what Green Mountain calls a "Solar-Slab." Stored heat subsequently helps heat the house at night and on cold days by radiation and a gentle assist from an upper-level blower. A hot-water pre-heater is contained within the system.

Thermo-Shutters, used on the inside of windows and sliding-glass patio doors, would further reduce heat loss at night. Not installed during the test period, it's estimated they would add 6 to 12 percent more efficiency.

The system is particularly complementary to wood-burning fireplaces and stoves, since the house is designed to redistribute heat generated in an isolated area. To reverse the system for summer cooling, night air is put into storage from midnight until 4 A.M., chilling the Solar-Slab. This prepares the slab to absorb the heat of the day, helping reduce the electrical demand on air-conditioning equipment.

Green Mountain homes are built from pre-cut and panelized parts, with design features so flexible that almost any home-builder's requirements can be met. All Model "N" Green Mountain homes are 16-feet-8½-inches wide and available in any length. All interior partitions are non-structural and therefore may be moved to suit any desired floor plan. There are 13 models, including seven in the "N" series, plus a garage. All of the homes are expandable and can be purchased in kit form, F.O.B. Royalton, Vermont. The Model N-38, shown here, with 1,264 square feet of living space, would cost an estimated $33,000 to build on a do-it-yourself basis, excluding land, septic system, well, and other site improvements. Allow an additional $6,000 for the 24×26-foot garage. Price for a contractor-built N-38 solar home and garage would come to around $49,000. Cost of the kits alone is approximately 40 percent of this price.

GREEN MOUNTAIN HOMES

### floor plan of the N-38 Solar Home

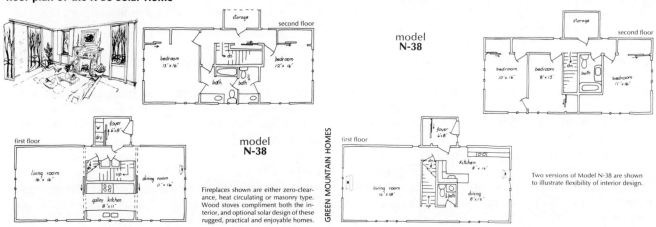

model N-38

Fireplaces shown are either zero-clearance, heat circulating or masonry type. Wood stoves compliment both the interior, and optional solar design of these rugged, practical and enjoyable homes.

model N-38

Two versions of Model N-38 are shown to illustrate flexibility of interior design.

GREEN MOUNTAIN HOMES

# Acorn Structures/Solar Capes

Acorn's solar houses take a straightforward "Cape" design from the past and bring it right up to tomorrow with a solar system that is integrated with the structural system of the house.

Acorn's solar houses have been especially designed to incorporate a solar system for space and domestic water heating, as well as to be energy-conserving houses in themselves. Heating systems in the center of Acorn's three Solar Cape models and passive solar heating through well-located windows are standard. Roof-mounted solar collectors are optional and may be installed when the house is built or at a later date.

The buildings have been designed so that solar collectors can be housed on the southerly side, yet broad expanses of south-facing glass have been maintained. The overhangs shade the glass when the sun is high in the summer, but allow the sun to heat the living space in the winter. Heating-system return ducts distribute this sun-warmed air from the south side and from the high cathedral spaces to the rest of the house. This prevents rooms with substantial passive solar gain from becoming overheated.

Standard construction specifies maximum insulation in walls, roof, and floors. Double insulating glass is used throughout, and windows and doors are tightly weather-stripped. Acorn's solar designs minimize windows on the north exposures, maximize south-facing glass with protective overhangs for summer sun, and locate the major living areas to benefit from the southerly exposure. Bedrooms and corridors are located on the northerly sides or in levels of the house where they can be separately zoned and regulated at lower temperatures. Chimneys are internal so that their heat loss to the outside is minimized. Entries are designed so that they can protect the living areas from direct influx of cold air.

Acorn has worked out a straightforward "Cape" design with a 47-degree roof pitch (an Acorn standard) for orientation of the collectors. Where the site dictates a house with a lower-pitched roof or an orientation and plan that makes it unfeasible to put collectors on the house, Acorn recommends the use of a detached "solar garage" for collectors.

Acorn's Sunwave collectors are built to serve as roofing panels, as well as collectors. They are made in a large 4×20-foot size to minimize piping connections, flashing, and jointing. Collector plates absorb the energy of the sunlight and this heat is transferred to water circulated from a basement storage tank. It takes several days of sun to fully "charge" the insulated, 2,200-gallon water tank, but enough energy to heat a house for several days can be stored in it.

Collected and stored heat is delivered to the house by pumping the warm storage water through a coil (like an auto radiator) placed in the duct of the warm-air heating system. Heat is controlled by a two-stage thermostat. Air moving past the coil is warmed by the water and heats the house until the thermostat is satisfied. If the storage water is not warm enough to satisfy the thermostat, the house will cool until the second-stage contact closes. This turns on the back-up furnace, which runs until the second stage is satisfied.

Domestic hot water gets its heat from the system by passing the supply to a conventional hot water tank through a 40-gallon pre-heating tank submerged in the storage water. In the non-house-heating months, sufficient energy is collected to carry almost all of the water-heating load.

The houses themselves, which come in 1,950, 2,300, and 2,900-square-foot plans, can be bought as erected shells, rough-finished, or finished houses. Erected-shell prices for Acorn's Solar Capes start at around $45,000. See pages 128–29 for other Acorn structures.

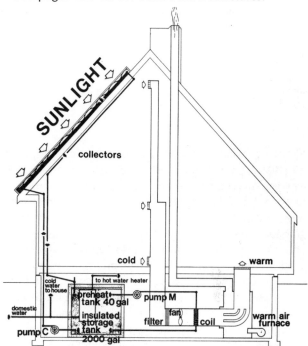

section view showing workings of the solar system in a Solar Cape

**floor plan of an Acorn Solar Cape**

**GENERAL DESCRIPTION**
32' x 40'
1964 sq. ft.
2 levels and attic
4 bedrooms
3 baths
Full foundation

## SOLAR CAPE 1950

The Solar Cape 1950 proves that an efficiently planned house can include many attractive details — a welcoming entry way which is formal and at the same time next to the kitchen; a 26 foot long living/dining room with the dining area defined and accented by plants and a cathedral ceiling. The high cathedral space collects air warmed by the sun for distribution throughout the house by the duct system. The exterior is highlighted by recesses and projections that reflect both function and pleasing design.

UPPER LEVEL

LOWER LEVEL

**SOLAR CAPES 1950 - 2300**
Included as standard on these models are items which are options on other Acorn houses:
½ x 6' clapboard siding or pine boards
Bird Architect 70 shingles
Oak stair and balcony rails
Oak shelves in the family-dining room divider
Pull down attic stair.

ACORN STRUCTURES, INC.

# GETTING STARTED

No matter what type of house you want to build, there are many things that must be done before you take delivery of the kit at the building site. With unimproved land, trees may have to be cleared and stumps removed, a driveway or road laid out. The land may have to be graded. If the site does not have access to town water and a community sewer line, a well must be dug and a septic system designed. Even with an improved subdivision lot, preliminary arrangements have to be made for sewer and water hookups. Arrangements must also be made to have electricity, and possibly natural gas, brought to the site. And then there's the matter of financing.

But even before all that, the place to start is at the municipal or county office which has the responsibility for issuing building permits. It's here that you'll learn whether or not the project is acceptable under applicable zoning and building codes. You might be restricted in how you use the site and may have to comply with unforeseen size, style, and setback requirements. There also may be limitations on the work that an owner can do—with or without supervision by a licensed professional.

This is a preliminary dialogue. You're not ready to apply for a building permit. You can't do that until you have a set of working drawings or engineering blueprints in hand to file with the application. Building codes apply to all aspects of construction and you may eventually have to provide the specifics on everything from footings to roofing materials. Frost depth, snow loads, fire codes, and a score of other local factors determine the minimum acceptable construction standards.

The construction materials provided with most packaged houses meet or exceed FHA minimum standards, so you aren't likely to get into a code conflict on that score. Local code problems more often involve the mechanical systems. It's here that you may have to bring in professional help, whether you want to or not. In many communities, there's not only a building or structural code, but separate codes covering electrical, plumbing, and heating systems, with installation permits often issued only to licensed professionals.

Some localities, however, do allow you to do your own electrical work, but not the plumbing. In other places, it's the other way around. In less-populated areas, building codes often are non-existent or not enforced, and a building permit may be only a formality, routinely issued by the town clerk. In this case, the responsibility for a safe house rests entirely with the owner, and we don't recommend that any work be done that would not be acceptable under a recognized national code, such as the One-and-Two-Family Dwelling Code or the National Electrical Code.

Before ordering a kit, make a careful estimate of the amount of money you expect to spend on each phase of the project, from preparing the foundation to final landscaping. Total all the additional expenditures that will be required, for finishing materials, heating, plumbing, etc. The kit may represent only a fraction of the total cost of building the house when you figure in the allocations for bringing in utilities, providing for waste disposal, and adding appliances and other furnishings. Is this a manageable sum—whether from cash on hand, loans or future income—paying as you go?

With some kit manufacturers, you have to place your order well in advance of the desired delivery date, particularly if you want delivery during the early summer months, which is a popular time for do-it-yourself building. Order far enough in advance, though, and you sometimes can take advantage of discounts granted when the mills are less busy. You'll be required to make a percentage down payment, usually 25 percent of the kit price, to secure the order and establish a firm delivery date. The balance will be payable on delivery—unless, of course, a deferred payment program has been worked out with the manufacturer.

You'll probably need at least four sets of working drawings or blueprints. These can be obtained from most manufacturers in advance of placing a kit order, with the cost deductible from the kit price if followed up with a purchase. One set of drawings, including specifications, floor plans, and elevations, is needed when you file for the building permit. Another is needed for the lender who will consider your application for a loan. Others will be needed if you seek bids from contractors or subcontractors. You'll also need a set for yourself.

If you haven't already purchased your working drawings, you should receive them within a week or two following the receipt of your kit order, plus a construction guide. Study this material carefully. If you don't plan to hire a general contractor, who is normally responsible for the total construction of the house, you'll have to work out a detailed schedule. What you will do. What others will do. And when. You have to coordinate the project so that nothing gets held up because one stage of the work did not get completed in time. Even so, there will be crises: a bottleneck caused by a lack of materials; or work that does not meet with the approval of the building inspector.

If you're going to be your own general contractor and subcontract some or all of the work, you better have a good understanding of what a general contractor does. You're going to have to buy the needed building materials not included with the kit, see to it that deliveries are made on time, line up the carpenters, roofers, electricians, and other subcontractors to do the various jobs. You're going to have to be on hand much of the time to see that work gets done and gets done right. With a 9-to-5 job and not much vacation time, this sort of supervision can be difficult over the three to six months or more the job may require before the house is ready to be lived in. Possibly your spouse could take over the role when you're not available.

If you don't feel confident enough to tackle some of the work involved, be assured that most carpenters, electricians, and other workers reach their skill peak after working on only three or four projects, long apprenticeships notwithstanding. And if you don't think a non-professional can tackle such things as plumbing, wiring, and heating systems, just drop into any building supply outlet and talk with a salesman. An enormous volume of business is done today in electrical, plumbing, and heating systems packaged, together with detailed instructions, for installation by do-it-yourselfers.

Once you have the financing, the kit ordered, the permits, and the subcontractors lined up, it's time to break ground. With a kit house, preparation of the foundation almost always is the owner's responsibility. And it should be completed in advance of the kit delivery, following specifications provided by the manufacturer.

Basically, there are four types of foundation: piers, slab, crawl space, and basement. Don't make a decision here without first checking into local customs and practices as they apply to the type of house you plan to build. The type of foundation in common use is usually based on past experience and cost comparisons.

Wood or concrete pier foundations are the simplest and least expensive to install. One drawback with piers, at least in northern climates, is that the floor needs to be well insulated, and if sufficient insulation hasn't been built in, it can be difficult to add after the house is up.

For concrete slab-on-grade—a concrete floor at ground level—it is important that the land fall sharply away from the level of the foundation to prevent flooding. With a slab foundation, the utilities usually are placed in the area where the basement stairwell would have gone. Plumbing should be roughed in before the floor is poured.

A crawl-space foundation is a perimeter foundation wall ranging from 30 to 40 inches in height. An enclosed crawl space is not difficult to insulate, provides useful storage space, and allows access to below-the-floor heating ducts, wiring, and plumbing.

A basement calls for a continuous foundation wall of reinforced poured concrete or concrete blocks, and a poured concrete floor below ground level, to give a ceiling height of at least 7 feet. Laying up masonry blocks shouldn't be too difficult for the owner-builder, but poured concrete is tricky. With poured concrete you also need to erect wall forms, and it's probably to your advantage to bring in a subcontractor with the necessary materials here.

If you don't need a basement, and fewer and fewer houses are being built with one, a crawl space is recommended with most types of construction. In some areas, particularly the warmer climates, concrete slabs are more common, but wood floor joists make for a warmer, more comfortable floor.

Where you build, though, does influence the choice of foundation. In the South, less than 20 percent of the houses being built today include a basement. In the West, only about 29 percent include a basement. In the Northeast, however, it's 69 percent. And in the North Central region, 81 percent include a basement.

There's a good answer for this. With any type of foundation, you first must pour your concrete footings. These must rest on natural, undisturbed soil below the frost line, conforming in depth and dimension to local building codes. In different parts of the country, extreme frost may range from 5 to 90 inches. Where a foundation depth of 5 feet or more is needed, it is quite economical to include a partial or full basement. It's also often practicable when building on a slope. It might add several thousand dollars to the cost of the house, but it's the cheapest space you can build.

Most packagers include details on preparing different types of foundations in their construction guides. Choose to suit your budget, needs, and the terrain. When it comes to digging, pick and shovel can't begin to match machine digging. Save time and lower-back pains by subcontracting major excavation work to a subcontractor with the necessary earth-moving equipment. He can do in hours what might take you weeks. Trenching for water and sewer lines or a septic system can be done at the same time.

The foundation should be completed before the kit arrives. Allow time for concrete to set before construction begins. The components of most kit houses are delivered via one or more 40-foot flatbed trailers. Check the route to the building site. Are there any bridges that won't permit the passage of what could be a 40-ton load? Unloading the materials usually is the responsibility of the customer, and you'll generally need a few helpers. With log houses, a forklift can be a big help, though some of the log manufacturers make deliveries with loader-equipped trailers. The ground should be prepared with straw or dunnage to keep the stock clean. Use tarps or heavy plastic to protect the piles of building materials after delivery and during construction.

You risk losing your house even before you start if you don't have insurance coverage against job hazards and accidents or other liabilities. Coverage is needed from the moment the kit is delivered until the house is completed. Do-it-yourselfers will need public-liability and property-damage coverage. Your insurance broker can also work out a package to cover losses from fire, vandalism, or malicious mischief, increasing as the building progresses. Make sure that any contractors or subcontractors engaged have workmen's compensation coverage.

When can you move in? In rural areas, it's often possible to move into a shell and camp out while you finish the job. In built-up areas, a certificate of occupancy may be required. Often this is not issued until after the building department's final inspection. To move up your move-in date, treat the project from the start as an "expandable," with the finishing of an upper or lower floor deferred. You can then usually take occupancy as soon as the "essentials" are in.

# WATER SUPPLY

A piece of land, no matter how splendid the view is from it, makes a poor homesite unless there's a convenient source of dependably pure water to meet household needs. In built-up suburban areas, there's usually a city water main or other existing supply system to which new residences can be hooked up without having to lay an unreasonable amount of pipe. But with most country property, the question of a safe and ample water supply needs to be answered *before* you put any money into building.

If the property borders on a lake, a large pond, or a stream that doesn't run dry in the summertime, it shouldn't be too difficult to tap such a body of water. But bear in mind that these sources are readily pollutable, receiving surface drainage without natural filtration, and that a clear stream can turn muddy after a heavy rain. The necessary hardware for tapping a lake, pond, or stream, however, can be a lot less expensive than the cost of drilling a well. The outlay might not run to more than $250—for a pump, storage tank, and pipe, run far enough and deep enough to avoid winter freeze-ups. On top of that, you'd have to figure the cost of any needed filtration or purification equipment.

Where the property in question is separated from a possible source of household water by intervening property, you'd have to make some arrangement, probably financial, with your neighbor and obtain an easement to run pipe across his land. This should be done through a lawyer so you'll have protection later should the two families start feuding for any reason.

A spring on the property can be as good as found money. The water, more often than not, will be refreshingly cool and safe to drink, having been naturally filtered through underground formations. Should it have an unpleasant taste due to the presence of sulphur or other dissolved minerals, this usually can be corrected with simple charcoal filtration. The quality of the water can be further improved at the source by removing the decaying vegetation and silt from the pit, screening the outlet pipe, and digging a ditch to keep drainage water away from the spring.

The biggest drawback with a spring is that, unless located at a higher elevation than the house, the pressure behind the flow rarely is sufficient to permit direct piping to kitchen and bathroom fixtures. The slow rate of flow requires a water-storage system, such as a large cistern in the basement, and a pump to provide pressure upstairs. If the spring doesn't flow year-round, don't bother with it.

A well is the usual—and most satisfactory—solution to the water-supply problem. Even where you have a municipal system that you can hook up to, it's often cheaper to have your own waterworks. According to the Water Systems Council, with his own well, a suburban-home or vacation-home owner can save up to $200 a year, based on the alternative of being tied into a community water system.

In many respects, searching for ground water is like drilling for oil. You need not only expertise, but a great deal of luck. The county agent, as well as the zoning and planning boards, can give you some useful information on such things as the probable depth to water-bearing strata, fluctuations in the ground water table, and the likely purity and mineral content of any water that you might find. Neighboring wells offer some guidance but no assurance of the depth at which an adequate water supply will be found. Talk to your neighbors, though. Find out how deep they had to go and what problems they encountered, if any.

We don't put a whole lot of faith in dowsing. There's no scientific explanation for a twig of apple, peach, or maple, held in the hands of a dowser, pointing to water deep underground. Sometimes it works. More often it doesn't. Considering that only about one person in one thousand has any dowsing ability at all, we'd have to attribute what success with the forked twig we've seen to the laws of chance. Anyway, you're still going to need a licensed well-driller, at least for a deep well. He's far and away your best authority on ground water. A local well man will know where wells have failed, where they have succeeded. He can tell you the probable depth, as well as the anticipated yield and cost.

Dug, bored, and driven wells go no deeper than 50 feet. Anything over 50 feet would be a tubular or drilled well. To avoid contamination, a well should be located on the highest ground practicable, and the well casing should terminate above the ground. Shallow wells, under 25 feet, are found mostly in natural basins and valleys, where the ground water table is not far below the surface. The shallower the well, however, the more easily it can be contaminated. If you're planning a septic-tank drainage field, locate it at least 100 feet away from the well

A small lot won't do for home builders supplying their own water and sewage-disposal facilities. You need a minimum of 20,000 square feet. That's about half an acre.

Take your future requirements, such as family additions, into consideration when planning your well. A flow of eight to 10 gallons per minute should be adequate for the average household. One easy formula: the demand (capacity) in gallons per minute should equal the number of fixtures installed—toilets, sinks, shower, outside faucet, washing machine, etc.—but not less than the peak demand for the single most thirsty fixture. With fire protection and other needs in mind, the recommended minimum for *any* house is not less than five gallons per minute at 30 pounds of pressure. Supply and pressure must be at least that to operate most of today's water-using appliances.

Shallow wells can be dug for a few hundred dollars. Figure another $200 for a one-third-horsepower shallow-well piston pump and a galvanized-steel storage tank. Deep wells, four inches or more in diameter, cost from $6 to $12 per foot, and it's not at all unusual to go down 200 feet and more. Jet and submersible pumps for wells as deep as 300 feet run to around $300. There are no pat rules for the best type of pump for a given installation. Each type of pump has its advantages as well as limitations.

With residential wells, you need a pump, a pressure/storage tank, and control devices for automatic operation. To provide a smooth flow of water in the typical modern home, you need a tank with a capacity of at least 42 gallons. Some pump tanks store air which can be compressed, so water can be drawn from the tank without the pump starting up each time water is drawn. The tank is factory-pre-charged with air that can't escape and the water is held in a collapsible vinyl bag. The amount of water that can be withdrawn from such tanks between pump starts is called the "draw down."

Including the drilling, the total cost of a deep well, pump and storage tank easily can run to $2,000. But today, is that an unreasonable price for an adequate supply of safe water? A pump should last 20 years; the well, twice that long. One caution: professional help is needed with the installation of a submersible pump and the hookup to the pressure tank.

The selection of the pump and the pressure system is also best done with the help of a pro. He can point you to such options as a bleeder system that drains water from the line between pump cycles. With this feature, you don't need to trench nearly as deep when you lay your pipe from the well to the house. You've avoided the freeze-up problem. With conventional systems, water pipe must be laid below the frost line. If you need to save on cost, do the trenching yourself.

Don't be afraid to tackle the inside-the-house water-system installation. Many local codes now permit the use of plastic pipe in place of more expensive brass or copper for interior cold-water lines. Some types of plastic pipe, such as CPVC, approved by the National Sanitation Foundation for drinking water, are also suitable for hot-water lines at temperatures up to 180 degrees. Most codes, though, often woefully behind advances in technology, continue to specify copper for hot-water lines.

With plastic pipe, you don't have to do any threading or soldering. Solvent cement is used to join pipe to fittings. You can install a sink, water heater, or clothes washer using just a saw, sandpaper, and knife. Try to keep plumbing runs short, with a minimum of bends and as few fittings as possible. Tees and elbows increase the friction of flow and reduce water pressure.

To improve water from whatever source for domestic use, you may want to install a sediment or taste-and-odor filter, either in the main supply line after it enters the house, or possibly for a single cold-water faucet only. Cartridge-type taste-and-odor filters for use ahead of a single cold-water faucet cost as little as $20. Replacement filters, good for about six months, cost under $5.

Do not confuse taste-and-odor filters with water purification. If the water as it comes into your house is not 100 percent safe to drink, the county agent or a well-drilling contractor can recommend a chlorinator or other water-treatment equipment to remove impurities and other unwanted substances. Have the water supply checked for purity at least once a year—and certainly before you begin using it. The cost for chemically testing a sample of water comes to around $10, a small price to pay to ensure your family's health.

# SEWAGE DISPOSAL

The sewage-disposal problem can be another key factor in determining where you build. Anyone planning to build in an outlying area where hookup to a municipal or community sewer line is not possible is going to need his own private sewage-disposal system. Concern for the ecology having barred the construction of new cesspools almost everywhere, the most common solution to the rural sewage-disposal problem today is a closed septic tank, buried in the ground, with a subsurface leaching field or a drywell for dispersal of the effluent.

Not all land, however, is sufficiently porous to support such a system. Indeed, much of the acreage sold in questionable land deals is not. If the soil is largely clay or hardpan, you're not going to be able to install the common-type septic system and may have to look elsewhere for a homesite. Before you put any money into construction, or country property, for that matter, have a civil engineer or other qualified person run a soil percolation test on the property. The test will cost around $100 and consists of digging six or more holes, filling them with water, and noting precisely how long it takes the surrounding soil to absorb the water. The ground moisture should be at or near its wet-season peak when the test is made.

Local sanitation codes, which often exist even where construction codes do not, will also require that the property be large enough to support a septic system. There are restrictions, too, as to how close the septic system can be to your house, property lines, and any body of water not entirely within your property.

While you might be able to do some of the digging yourself, a septic system should, and in most locales must, be designed and installed by an expert. When a septic system goes wrong, you've got a headache that'll take more than a couple of Anacin to cure.

The septic tank can be either steel or concrete. If you want some advice here, concrete tanks tend to last a lot longer than steel ones. For a two-bedroom or smaller house, tank capacity should be a minimum of 750 gallons. Add another 250 gallons for each additional bedroom. These capacities allow for the use of garbage disposals and washing machines. Costs, with installation, depend much on local codes, available labor, and soil conditions. The range would be from around $600 to $2,000.

The household waste pipe leads to the septic tank and a second pipe leads from the tank to a distribution box. Parallel lines of large-diameter perforated plastic pipe or clay draintile, set approximately two feet below grade in beds of gravel six to eight feet apart, lead away from the distribution box. Back-filled with soil and planted with grass, this is the leaching field. The size of the leaching field generally is based on the number of bedrooms in a house and the absorption rate of the soil. For a typical two-bedroom house and a "moderate" soil absorption rate, you need roughly 200 feet of pipe or tile.

After waste reaches the septic tank, it is attacked by sewage-digesting bacteria. This stage of the system is anaerobic, meaning the microorganisms ingesting the waste can thrive in the absence of air or free oxygen. They slowly reduce solids to gases, liquids, and sludge. The gases are vented harmlessly into the atmosphere via the house soil stack and the effluent drains off through the outlet pipe and is dispersed into the soil via the leaching field. The sludge, a fraction of the original volume of the waste, settles at the bottom of the watertight tank and must be pumped out every three to five years—an event you'll not soon forget.

Do not allow cigarette filters or the plastic in disposable diapers to enter the septic system. The bacteria with which the tank is seeded work only on biodegradable substances.

Leaching fields should not be laid with the lines sloping more than 15 degrees downhill or in low-lying areas where the ground water table is close to the surface. Serial distribution, with the leach lines laid on the contour, is necessary with most sloping fields or in fields where there is a change in the soil type.

A drywell or seepage pit is an alternative to leach lines. Constructed usually from porous cinder blocks and set atop a deep bed of gravel, a drywell should be used only where soil percolation is rated moderate or better. Because of the greater depth required for seepage, soil depth also is more critical here than it is with a leaching field.

Aerobic systems are not to be confused with *anaerobic* systems. Unlike the conventional septic system, which excludes outside oxygen from the waste tank, fresh air is bubbled continuously through the waste in an aerobic system. A different strain of bacteria takes over here, one that thrives on oxygen and works on waste far more efficiently. The effluent is odorless and relatively harmless when it leaves the tank, reducing the absorption field needs. The system is now finding acceptance in most states. In parts of Pennsylvania, for example, when an aerobic system is used, codes permit a one-third reduction in the size of the drainage area required for an anaerobic system. This is on the conservative side. Some experts hold that aerobic systems permit a *two*-thirds reduction in soil absorption requirements. The cost of an aerobic system, installed, ranges from $1,350 to $3,000.

Most codes now permit the use of plastic pipe for inside as well as outside drain lines, which makes the installation of interior waste pipes a good deal less difficult than in the past. The essentials, apart from the fixtures, include a 4-inch-diameter soil stack, which leads from the toilet to the septic tank or sewer line, and one or more vent pipes to the roof to prevent gases from building up pressure in the system. Unlike the freshwater system, which is pressurized, the drainage system works by gravity. All drains slope toward the stack. Vents must slope away from the stack. The drainage system starts at each fixture with a section of curved pipe called a trap. The main purpose of the trap is not to catch rings and other objects that slip into the drain, but to provide a water barrier to prevent sewage odors from escaping into the house.

That, in brief, covers the more common waste-disposal systems. Depending on your situation, however, you may want to consider a waste-disposal system that *doesn't* require a sewer line or an extensive drainage field. This could be the case where you have more bedrock or tree roots than soil, or where the permeability of the soil will not permit an absorption field.

For a vacation home or hideaway that doesn't get a lot of visitors, or that doesn't have running water, a portable, self-contained toilet is one solution. These generally come with a bacteriostat to render waste reasonably sanitary and inoffensive and are the type of toilets used today in thousands of self-contained recreation vehicles. Some of the newest portable recirculating-type toilets, charged with as little as four gallons of water and bacteriostat, are good for 80 to 90 flushes before the detachable holding tank has to be taken to a dumping station. Units designed to be permanently installed have a provision for piping waste to a larger holding tank or to a pumpout facility. Recirculating-type toilets, some of which come with electric flush pumps, cost from $100 to $250.

A second alternative would be an oxidizing or dry sanitary toilet, which works without water, chemicals, or a holding tank. A dry sanitary toilet is simply an incinerator enclosed in a functional housing that keeps the seat and all exterior surfaces comfortably cool at all times. It disposes of wastes by way of a forced-air gas flame that operates only after the lid has been closed and a heat shield moves into place. Cycles can be interrupted at any time for toilet use. When the lid is raised, a fan automatically vents the system. Installation is similar to a gas dryer, using an electrical connection, gas inlet, and a vertical flue outlet. There is no maintenance other than weekly removal of the sterile ash. These toilets operate on bottled gas as well as piped-in natural gas and cost around $400 and up.

An even more intriguing device for waterless disposal of human wastes is the Clivus Multrum organic waste-treament system. This Swedish-designed system transforms human waste and kitchen scraps into humus, without unsightliness or odor. Clivus Multrum translates to "inclining compost room," and it is just that: a compost heap set at a precisely calculated angle inside an irregularly shaped Fiberglas box measuring roughly $4 \times 5 \times 9$ feet. Installed in the basement and with vertical chutes connecting the chamber to the toilet and a kitchen refuse opening, wastes fed into the system mix with a "seed" layer of garden soil and grass clippings and move down the slope at glacial speed. Toilet wastes enter at the high end, pass through the kitchen wastes, and are thoroughly decomposed by the time the residue reaches the storage compartment two to four years later. Natural convection ensures that the process is essentially aerobic and that the bathroom and kitchen are kept free of odors at all times. With the moderate heat of the compost reaction, up to 95 percent of the sewage goes up the vent as carbon dioxide and water vapor, the main products of the bacterial decomposition. The end product of this mini eco-system is safe enough for use in gardens. The process, being continuous, will generate three to 10 gallons of humus-like soil per person per year.

Eliminating the need for flushing cuts household water use by 40 percent. With toilet wastes separated from household waste water, the remaining "gray water" is much more easily treated. A Clivus Multrum toilet system with a large enough capacity to serve three persons year-round, with allowance for visitors, costs around $1,795 with all hardware necessary for most installations.

# ELECTRIC SYSTEM

Wiring the house is the next step after the shell is up, partitions have been framed, and the plumbing has been roughed in. It's no more difficult than good carpentry, but most amateur builders would sooner fondle a rattlesnake than tackle the electric system. Don't let the fact that you've never grasped the difference between an ohm and an ampere stop you. There's no big mystery to installing a convenience outlet and a wall switch. If you can do that, you have nothing to worry about here. You're not handling live wires. All elements of the system are dead until the completed work, whether done by you or by a licensed electrician, has been approved by a building inspector. Not until then can the utility company connect the service line.

In some areas, strict building codes require that the planning and installation of the electric system be done by a licensed professional. But where you have the option of doing some or all of the work yourself, a visit to the utility company offices would be a good first step. Take along a floor plan of the house and a list of the appliances and other plug-ins you'll be using. One of the company's engineers can then tell you what strength service you'll need.

For a vacation home or small dwelling where the peak demand will not exceed 13,800 watts—for lights, water heater, refrigerator, water pump, and TV, say—a 60-ampere system would be sufficient. The standard for most small- and medium-sized houses today, though, is 100 amperes—and 230 volts, for a maximum of 23,000 watts. There's a simple equation that applies here: amperes times volts equals watts. In larger houses, and where you have central air conditioning and/or electric heating, 150- to 400-ampere systems are needed.

The utility company engineer can help you avoid the common problems of inadequate voltage and amperage. He can acquaint you with the National Electrical Code and applicable HUD-FHA Minimum Property Standards. He also can tell you how much it will cost to have electricity brought to your site. At one time, utilities absorbed this expense when the customer was within reasonable distance of an existing power line. But today, you'll likely be charged for every utility pole and section of service line required to bring electricity to you. In addition, you may have to pay the cost of cutting down any trees or branches that interfere with or pose a threat to the line. With remote installations, this could prove to be prohibitively expensive until there is additional demand for extension of a power line to the area.

Your electric system begins at the "service entrance," which is where the service line, either overhead via poles or underground via conduit from the street, comes into the house and passes through the meter socket to the entrance-panel box. The entrance panel should include a switch that can be thrown to cut off all house current in the event of an emergency or when work is to be done on the system.

From the entrance panel, electricity is distributed to various lighting circuits and individual appliances. With 60-ampere service, there will be six to eight branch circuits; with 100 amperes, 12 to 16 branch circuits; and so on. Each circuit has a fuse or, more likely, circuit breaker that will cut off the flow of electricity to that circuit automatically should there be an overload or short in the line. Circuit breakers are designed to accept momentary start-up overloads, but turn themselves off when an otherwise excessive amount of electricity, whether due to a faulty appliance or crossed wires, passes through them. Once the trouble has been diagnosed and corrected, the switch is simply thrown again to restore the circuit.

General circuits serving separate areas of the house connect to permanently installed lighting fixtures, such as ceiling lights, and wall outlets into which lamps and low-wattage appliances can be plugged. Providing 1,800 watts of 115-volt power, and protected with a 15-ampere circuit breaker, wiring for these circuits is two-wire type, No. 14 wire or larger, with an insulation covering. The National Electrical Code and the FHA call for a minimum of three watts of power per square foot of floor area for general circuits. Five watts per square foot is a better measure, though, for convenience and to allow for possible expansion later. For a 1,500-square-foot house, this would mean three, but preferably five, general circuits.

Special circuits for the operation of countertop and individual small appliances, such as a garbage disposal or a built-in bathroom heater, provide 2,400 watts of 115-volt power and are protected with 20-ampere circuit breakers. Three-wire circuits are needed for high-wattage appliances such as electric ranges (a typical range can use 10,000 watts) and the larger-capacity air conditioners. The wire for these circuits ranges from No. 12 to No. 6 in size (the smaller the number, the larger the wire) and may carry 230 volts. Protection is usually provided with two side-by-side circuit breakers bridged together.

The use of rigid steel pipe, with insulated wire drawn through it after the pipe has been installed, is the most expensive way of running wire. It meets all codes, though, and is the way building inspectors would prefer to see it done. But non-metallic-sheathed cable, often called "Romex," is far more widely used for residential wiring today. It is simpler and faster to install than conduit and meets the wiring standards of the National Electrical Code and the One-and-Two-Family Dwelling Code.

The metal conduit most often used today is thin-wall steel conduit. It's easier to work with than rigid pipe. It looks a lot like spiral-wound BX cable, except that the insulated wire, as with rigid pipe, is drawn through the conduit after installation. Armored cable, or BX, no longer is widely used in new construction.

Electrical installations are done more or less backward. One of the first steps is to mount the outlet boxes, anchoring them to metal hangers, masonry, and studding in such a way that the outlet receptacle, when installed, will be flush with the finished wall. Be generous with those outlets. A good rule to follow is FHA's requirement that no point of usable wall perimeter be farther than six feet from a duplex three-prong grounding outlet. Since 1960, the National Electrical Code and FHA have required that all outlet receptacles be the grounding type, designed to accept a two- or a three-prong plug. A 230-volt line requires a special receptacle that will not accept a standard two- or three-prong plug.

Switches should be placed to permit walking into any area of the house, lighting the way, and extinguishing the lights without having to stumble about in the dark. You should be able to control stairway lights from both upstairs and down. This can be done with three-way switches. In the kitchen, the bathroom, and the laundry room, lighting fixtures should work by a switch, not by a chain. Metal pull chains never should be used where there is the possibility of a wet floor. Care must also be taken when installing cable or conduit to preclude the possibility of nails or other fasteners striking the wiring when you install the wall materials.

What's all this going to cost? There's no formula that applies here, but Sears sells an electric wiring kit with all the materials needed to wire a 1,500-square-foot house for around $400. The kit includes 2,000 feet of wire, 65 switch boxes, 65 wall plates, 47 duplex outlets, 14 four-inch outlet boxes, 66 feet of plastic tape, 15 cable connectors, 24 wire connectors, 300 nail straps, and 79 grounding pigtails. Sears' service-entrance kits, with metal conduit and circuit-breaker-type entrance panels, are priced at $99.95 (100 amperes) and $179.95 (200 amperes). Detailed installation instructions are included.

One of the options to bringing in electricity is to generate your own. A generator also is a good idea in snow country, where it's not unusual to have several power failures each winter. A 3½-hp, 1,200-watt, single-voltage generator for emergency standby power could operate the furnace fan and house lights. A power plant with this capacity costs around $250 and up. To operate the furnace fan, house lights, refrigerator, freezer, and sump pump, you'd need something on the order of a 6-hp, 2,600-watt unit, which would cost around $400. From here, especially if you include space heating electrically, it's on up the price scale. Some power plants operate on diesel fuel, but most operate on gasoline and natural or propane gas. By nature, they're thirsty beasts. A 16-hp, 7,000-watt generator, costing around $1,300, provides enough power to run a whole house, but it can easily consume a gallon and a half of fuel every 60 minutes.

Other alternatives to bringing in electricity from a utility would include wind- and water-powered generators. There's also solar energy, but at this stage it's at best a supplement to a conventional power source and pretty much limited to heating water and space. A solar system that will generate electrical energy on a practical basis, providing sufficient energy for heating, lighting, and refrigeration, may still be light-years away.

# HEATING

There's been a return to centrally located fireplaces and chimneys. They're more energy-efficient than fireplaces and chimneys that are part of an outside wall.

The temptation today is to wait until the house is up before deciding, based on a last pained look at escalating fuel costs and fuel availability, how to heat it. This might work out all right if you settle for a free-standing fireplace or a wood-burning stove. But with most whole-house-heating systems, there's often a considerable amount of work that is best done during the roughing-in stages, before the walls and floors are closed. Forced-warm-air systems, for one, require extensive ducting, which, after partition framing, gets priority over plumbing and wiring. With a masonry chimney, there are major structural considerations that begin with the foundation.

Heating is very much a part of the house plan. The decisions that have to be made here should not be postponed. Your needs will, of course, depend on whether the house is intended for year-round or seasonal use. But you should also anticipate future needs—a change from vacation to retirement living or other full-time use of the house.

There are four basic types of house-heating systems. By far the most common are forced-warm-air systems, which have as their heart a furnace in which air is generally heated by an oil or gas burner, with natural-gas-fired equipment predominating in new homes. The heated air is then blown through metal or composition ducts to floor and wall registers in the different rooms of the house. In rural and suburban areas not served by a utility gas line, your choice of fuels would be narrowed. Natural-gas furnaces can be adjusted to burn propane, but using bottled gas to operate a central heating system is an expensive alternative.

Since ducting is necessary for both forced-warm-air systems and central air conditioning, you might have an added inducement to go with this type of system and use the same duct installation for both heating and cooling.

The ducting in this case should be of the somewhat larger capacity required with central air conditioning. You can't add central air conditioning later and expect ducts scaled for forced-warm-air heating to serve as effectively.

Circulating-hot-water systems begin with a boiler in which water is heated to around 180 degrees. A small pump, or circulator, sends the heated water through a labyrinth of pipes to room radiators, convectors, baseboard circuits, or coils embedded in concrete-slab floors. Forced-hot-water heating systems, depending on the design of the furnace, may use one or more of a variety of fuels, including oil, gas, coal, and wood. One disadvantage of circulating-hot-water systems is their vulnerability to freeze-ups if the house is closed in cold weather. Unless antifreeze has been added, the system must be drained, which could make it a poor choice for a weekend ski lodge.

Thermostatically controlled electric-baseboard heating is the most efficient of all house-heating systems, but with soaring electric rates it has lost some of its attractiveness. It may still be your best bet, though, for a vacation home or where moisture can be a problem. The thermostats can be set just high enough to keep the house dry and free of frost during an absence. Another advantage: electric-baseboard or wall-heating units allow zoned heating, which means bedrooms can be closed off during the day and other areas heated as needed for normal family comfort. At night, the bedrooms can be warmed and the rest of the house set for a lower temperature. A well-insulated house is required, though, for electric heating to be at all economical.

Heat pumps, which also depend on electricity, are gaining acceptance despite their often high cost of operation. In cool weather, they warm the house; in warm weather, they cool it. The distribution system is the same as with forced warm air, both heating and cooling from a central system. A heat pump is a more efficient method of combining a conventional forced-warm-air heating system with central air conditioning. In this case, the system is an integral one and runs only off electricity. The performance of a heat pump depends on the outside temperature. Where the average winter temperature is 30 to 40 degrees F., it has a considerable advantage over a conventional electric furnace. It loses that edge at about 15 degrees or less.

Mention should be made of propane or LP gas, which is a traditional part of country living. It is used as a fuel for heating and cooking in many summer homes. One disadvantage: for safety's sake, the system has to be shut down completely during any absence of more than a few days. Flame failure or undetected leakage of propane can be a real hazard. The gas, which is 1.5 times heavier than air, tends to pool and an explosion can be set off by a spark.

There's more romance than BTU's in a cozy, log-burning fireplace. Unaided, a fireplace is about the least efficient way there is of heating a house, with up to 95 percent of the heat lost. But it's part of the American home-owning dream, and we, for one, wouldn't want to build a house without one. It would be foolish, though, to attempt to build a fireplace and chimney without detailed knowledge of what's involved.

A masonry chimney, for one thing, is not something you can tack onto a house as an afterthought. It's the heaviest portion of the house and an integral part of the construction. You need a good footing for it, set below the frost line, with the base built up to near floor level. This part, at least, should be built at the same time as the foundation.

If you've never seen the inside of a chimney, there's some tricky engineering involved here, including a built-in smoke shelf to check cold air and aid the upward flow of smoke. Adequate protection from the hot chimney flue, using separation and insulation, is essential. The dimensions of the flue are also important. The flue should measure at least one-tenth the area of the fireplace opening. Even the height of the chimney-top extension is critical. Unless the flue top is at least two feet above the nearest ridge line or other part of the roof within 10 feet of the chimney, the chimney will not draw properly.

Fireplace building is an art, and done by professionals, you can pay $4,000 and more for a fireplace and chimney built of stone. An all-brick fireplace and chimney will cost about half what you'd pay for one built of stone. There are other, less expensive alternatives. One is to use a prefabricated metal chimney and a factory-built metal fire-box that you surround with a masonry or other noncombustible facing. A complete factory package, including a single-flued, double-

A Franklin-type stove keeps American Timber Homes' chalet cozy.

walled (with insulation between) chimney, should cost under $1,200.

If you're looking to heat more than the fireplace, there are prefabricated fireplaces with outlets that can be connected to ducts to carry the heated air to other areas of the house. You can further increase the efficiency of a fireplace with a hearth grille through which air for combustion is brought from outside the house. A fireplace needs lots of air to keep the fire glowing. If you're taking it from inside the house, you're also pulling in cold air through cracks around the doors and windows.

Least complicated and expensive would be a free-standing or wall-hung steel fireplace. These come with a porcelain-enamel finish and in a choice of colors. Most are conical, with integral hoods, and are fashioned with two layers of steel, with insulation between, so the exterior doesn't get too hot. They aren't much more efficient than a fireplace, but they add a nice ambience to a vacation home. Often sold as a package with a prefabricated triple-wall metal chimney and all the materials necessary to pass the chimney through the roof or an exterior wall, price for a free-standing fireplace package would run roughly from $400 to $700.

A free-standing fireplace should be set no closer than 36 inches to a combustible wall; 24 inches if a heat shield, required by some codes, is used. A non-combustible base is another requirement. This can be fashioned from bricks, slate, pebbles, or sand, surrounded by a frame of 2 × 4's set on edge.

Wood-burning heaters and stoves are making a vigorous comeback, as a supplement to a furnace or to replace it completely. While we can't picture getting romantic in front of one, they are many times more efficient than most fireplaces. Installation is the same as with a free-standing fireplace.

Back in 1743, Benjamin Franklin invented "an open stove for better warming of rooms." This is the Franklin stove, which opens to serve as a fireplace, and many versions of it are being sold today. Made of heavy steel and/or cast iron, a Franklin stove can be fully set up for under $500. Few heating devices work as well or as cheaply. They do, however, need frequent tending.

Even more popular, at least in the Northeast and other winter sports areas, are airtight, end-fired Scandinavian and Dutch stoves, also made of rugged cast iron. The Scandinavians, in particular, have made a science of stove design, and the front-end combustion system allows wood to burn slowly, like a cigar, over long periods without refueling. The object is to radiate heat into the room and not up the chimney. The imports are not cheap, selling for from $400 to $900, plus chimney installation.

You've also got to figure the cost of firewood, which today ranges from $40 to $150 a true cord (128 cubic

**The Jotul 118 will hold a fire all night. You can go 24 hours on only two stokings—the reason why the Norwegians call them "round burners."**

**Many free-standing fireplaces and stoves add more ambience than heat, but they're relatively simple to install and can provide a cheery glow.**

The home is Pacific Frontier Homes' Frontier IV and the elegantly styled stove in the corner is a Morso 1125. The Danish import sells for $730, but it is held to be three times more efficient than a Franklin stove, seven times more efficient than a masonry fireplace.

feet), depending on local supply conditions. If you've had no experience with firewood, seasoned hardwoods such as ash, oak, hard maple, hickory, beech, and black locust make the best fuels. Green hardwoods and softwoods such as fir and pine do not make good fuels. Some of these stoves will also burn hard coal. But many of them are designed to burn wood only. If you're looking to save money on furnace fuels, a wood stove may not be the answer.

With any heating-system installation, whether done by yourself or a heating contractor, have a building inspector check the work before you fire up.

the Morso 1125

# FINANCING KIT HOUSES

This book is not about buying country property or a building lot in suburbia. But since you can't put up a house without land, let's look briefly at ways to finance the purchase of undeveloped land or an improved building site, before getting into the financing of the house itself. For many young families, acquiring land is the key to the housing problem. Once you own a piece of land, it's often all the equity you need to swing a mortgage commitment or construction loan. With soaring land costs, anyone with a paid-for site these days is halfway home.

In acquiring undeveloped land, often the best source of financing is the seller. If he has held the property for more than one year and stands to realize a capital gain, there are tax advantages if he uses the installment method to report his gain, and the payments in the year of sale do not exceed 30 percent of the selling price. The exchange generally is effected with a "land sale contract," the buyer giving a cash down payment of from 5 to 30 percent and paying off the balance to the seller in annual installments at a mutually acceptable rate of interest.

Building lots often can be bought from land developers on much easier terms—as little as $50 down and $50 a month for 10 to 15 years. But a word of caution here: *never, never* buy property on which you have not set foot! Far too many of those tracts, usually bought into on the basis of a colorful prospectus by families planning ahead for their retirement years, are suited only for scorpions or alligators.

Make sure you are buying land on which you can build. There are millions of acres for which building permits never will be issued, primarily because the land doesn't have "percolation approval." The soil conditions are unfavorable for the installation of waste-disposal systems.

It's a fallacy that few financial institutions will lend money to private individuals for the purchase of land. This was the case up until a few years ago. But with good, reasonably accessible land almost certain to continue to increase in value, many banks today will lend up to 75 percent of the appraised value for even an unimproved homesite, for terms of up to five years to good credit risks. This means a buyer could acquire a $12,000 parcel with a down payment of $3,000. The payments on a five-year homesite mortgage would amount to slightly over $200 a month. At the end of five years, the buyer is in an advantageous position when applying for a construction loan from the same lender. And even before the land is paid for, he may be able to mortgage-out—that is, borrow enough to build his house and pay off the property, too.

With unimproved land, lending agencies are much more likely to listen to someone who plans to build in the very near future rather than someone who wants to buy land as an investment. Some banks will even require that a part of the land loan go into improving the land—with an access road, site clearing, or whatever.

Banks, as a rule, observe geographic boundaries in making loans. Your best bet is to deal with those banks and other lending institutions that are closest to the general area in which you intend to build. They will be familiar with the area's values. They may also know facts about the property that the seller might not disclose.

Once you have a clear title to the land, you can start looking into ways to finance the house. The simplest and least expensive way is to draw on your own resources (savings, cash value of life insurance, equity in other properties) and pay as you build. If you don't have the cash to build, you generally need two types of loans: a construction loan, and, later, a permanent mortgage on the completed house. Long-term mortgages on unbuilt houses are rare. A pile of pre-cut lumber is not the best collateral.

Not all urban bankers are familiar with the sweat-equity concept of building. But in suburban areas, lending institutions are seeing more and more demand for this type of financing and are coming into the market to provide it. If you can show that you're a good credit risk, and give detailed plans for your project, showing what you will do, what will be done by subcontractors, you should be able to get a conditional mortgage, which is a firm commitment for a permanent mortgage once the construction work has been satisfactorily completed. You would then get an interim "draw" loan, from the same or another bank, to buy the kit and additional materials and pay for any required labor during construction and into the finishing phases.

To apply for a standard construction loan, you must own your property free and clear and must submit to the bank detailed plans and cost estimates. For loan approval, you may be required to employ the services of a licensed general contractor, who would be committed by contract to build the house. This makes it somewhat more difficult for an owner to do very much of his own work. Since the contractor will be responsible for satisfactory completion of the work, the amount of the loan must reflect the cost of having the contractor do *all* the work. Most owners work out an arrangement with the contractor, however, to compensate them for the portion of the work they are able to do themselves.

When banks provide the construction money, they generally charge a fee, based on the amount borrowed, for processing the loan and to cover inspection of the building at different stages of construction. This is in addition to the going rate of interest on the loan. Again, those banks that are most likely to grant a construction loan are those commercially active in the general area in which you build. A Chicago banker isn't likely to give a mortgage on a lakeside retreat in Wisconsin. But check with your local bank, anyway. Any lender will favor a regular customer over a stranger, and the bank *may* be part of a group serving a wide area.

If you have only enough money at your disposal to pay for the basic kit, you might look for "short-term" money, such as a direct personal loan from a bank or credit union, to finish it off. Once the house is completed, you can then apply for traditional long-term financing to pay off your short-term notes. Personal loans command a higher rate of interest than mortgage loans, but then you can save on those construction-loan fees, which could more than offset the interest differential. You also have the same advantages here as when building with cash: you can take advantage of cash discounts, ranging from 2 to 10 percent, given by contractors and suppliers, and you can be your own general contractor.

If these methods of financing fall short of your needs, most manufacturers of kit houses stand ready to suggest other approaches, which may or may not include a temporary credit arrangement to get you over the hump. Remember that many of these companies have had a lot of experience helping other owner-builders. Very likely they or their representatives will have some acquaintance with lending institutions in the general area in which you plan to build and will work closely with the lender of your choice. Some will even provide you with a list of banks that have financed other kit-builders.

There are many factors to be considered here, of course, and the type of loan or mortgage for which you may qualify will depend on everything from the size and cost of the project to how much of the work you plan to do yourself. In developed areas, building codes may require that the house be built by a contractor. Still other units are offered *only* as dealer-erected shells. (At one time, virtually every shell-home manufacturer offered both temporary and long-term financing, at interest rates comparable to those charged by regular lending institutions. Some still do.) It also should be pointed out that mortgage loans on vacation houses usually run at a slightly higher rate of interest than you would pay on a primary residence, and the term of the loan is shorter—10 or 15 years, as opposed to 25, 30, or 35 years.

If you pour a fair amount of sweat equity into your house, however, chances are it will be worth considerably more than the total cost of the project, and a mortgage loan, enabling the initial financing to be repaid when the "essentials" of the house are completed, should be no problem. The fact that many of the houses built from kits are more energy efficient than conventional, stick-built houses makes them easy to resell and is becoming an important plus with lenders.

If you have a choice, shop for your mortgage as aggressively as you would for a new car. While most houses are financed with conventional mortgages, not all banks charge the same rate of interest. A quarter of a percentage point can mean thousands of dollars over the years. Conventional mortgages, as a rule, require a down payment of from 20 to 25 percent of the house's appraised value and are written for between 20 and 30 years. With FHA-insured loans, the minimum down payment on the first $25,000 is just 3 percent, and repayment periods are 30 to 35 years. VA-guaranteed loans, for eligible veterans, are written for from 25 to 30 years, and no-down-payment loans are possible. With FHA and VA loans, the federal government protects the lender from any losses. These loans have their attractions, but—catch 22—the delays and red tape involved have turned most bankers against them. A lot of banks just won't process applications for FHA and VA loans. If you plan to seek an FHA loan, bear in mind that the house must meet FHA Minimum Property Standards, which can be stricter than local building codes and apply not only to construction, but to design and location, as well.

There's one other type of loan you should know about. That's a FmHA loan. Not to be confused with FHA (the Federal Housing Administration), FmHA is the Farmers Home Administration. If you can't get other financing, you may qualify for a loan under this agency's direct-lending program. This "banker" of last resort grants loans at reduced rates of interest to low- and moderate-income families building or buying in sparsely populated areas. Generally, the loans, which are for up to 33 years, are made for smaller, no-frills houses, with from 800 to 1,200 square feet of living area. If you think you might qualify, talk to your county FmHA agent.

Of the three variables with any loan—the down payment required, the rate of interest and the length of the loan—the one with which you should be most concerned is the rate of interest. If you're going to be paying off the loan for the next 10 to 35 years, you want the lowest rate available. Going by the old rules of finance your grandpa may have taught you while bouncing you on his knee, you'd also make as big a down payment as you could manage and arrange to pay off the loan as quickly as possible. But times have changed and the dollar's been shot full of holes. With continuing inflation, you're better off making as *small* a down payment as possible and *stretching out* the loan. You'll be paying back borrowed money with cheaper, future dollars and likely taking tax deductions for the finance charges, as well. As any financial planner can tell you, cash, today, can be put to better use than pre-paying a home loan.

# Directory of Manufacturers

This directory includes pertinent sales and other information provided by various kit-house manufacturers. Although most companies will supply a home to any area of the country, keep in mind that the costs of long-distance shipping can cancel out some of the inherent advantages of kit-building. We've listed some of the more detailed literature available and for which, in most cases, there is a charge. But a query to any of the manufacturers should produce at least a free folder summarizing their houses in reply.

Acorn Structures, Inc.
Box 250,
Concord, Massachusetts 01742
Products: panelized package homes; solar homes and systems
Market: east of the Mississippi
Literature: planning and information kit, $5

AGI: The Shelter People
2001 Hammond Street,
Freedom Park,
Bangor, Maine 04401
Products: pre-cut and panelized geodesic domes; hexagons
Market: national
Literature: Omegadome catalog and paper scale model, $3; hexagon data package, $1

Air-Lock Log Co., Inc.
P. O. Box 2506,
Las Vegas, New Mexico 87701
Products: pre-cut log homes (hollowed pine logs)
Market: national
Literature: plans book, $2.50

The Aladdin Company
Bay City, Michigan 48706
Products: pre-cut and panelized homes
Market: east of the Rockies
Literature: catalog, 25¢

Alta Industries Ltd.
P. O. Box 88,
Halcottsville, New York 12438
Products: pre-cut log homes (white pine logs)
Market: Maine to Missouri
Literature: portfolio, $3

American Geodesic, Inc.
See AGI: The Shelter People

American Pioneer Buildings, Inc.
P. O. Box 69,
Milford, Virginia 22514
Products: panelized log homes (splined cedar half-logs)
Market: eastern states
Literature: cabin/home brochure, $2.50

American Timber Homes, Inc.
Escanaba, Michigan 49829
Products: panelized package homes
Market: east of the Rockies
Literature: brochure, $3.50

L. C. Andrew, Inc.
28 Depot Street,
South Windham, Maine 04082
Products: panelized log homes (northern white cedar)
Market: Northeast

Arkansas Log Homes, Inc.
Mena, Arkansas 71953
See Vermont Log Buildings, Inc.

Authentic Homes Corp.
P. O. Box 1288,
Laramie, Wyoming 82070
Products: pre-cut log homes (pine)
Market: national
Literature: plans book, $3

Beaver Log Homes
110 North Cleburn,
P. O. Box 1966,
Grand Island, Nebraska 68801
Products: pre-cut log homes (pine)
Market: national
Literature: plans book, $4.50

Bellaire Log Cabin Manufacturing Co.
P. O. Box 322,
Bellaire, Michigan 49615
Products: pre-cut log homes (white cedar split-logs)
Market: national

The Big Outdoors People, Inc.
26600 Fallbrook Avenue,
Wyoming, Minnesota 55092
Products: geodesic domes (hub and strut)
Market: national
Literature: The Dome Plan Book, $6; Alternate Living Systems Product Catalog, $1.50; Dome Flyer newsletter, $2.50

Blackstock Homes
2344 S.W. Spokane Street,
Seattle, Washington 98106

Products: pre-cut component homes
Market: Pacific Northwest, Alaska, and Hawaii
Literature: plans folder, $2

Boise Cascade
See Kingsberry Homes

Boyne Falls Log Homes, Inc.
Boyne Falls, Michigan 49713
Products: pre-cut and panelized log homes (cedar)
Market: national
Literature: portfolio, $3

Building Logs, Inc.
P. O. Box 300,
Gunnison, Colorado 81230
Products: pre-cut log homes (pine Lok-Logs)
Market: national

Can-Am Log Houses, Ltd.
P. O. Box 1297,
Waterloo, Quebec J0E 2N0
Products: pre-cut log homes (pine)
Literature: catalog, $1

Capp Homes
4525 Northpark Drive,
Colorado Springs, Colorado 80907
Products: pre-cut custom homes
Market: Midwest to far West
Literature: Capp Home Planning Guide, free

Carolina Log Buildings, Inc.
Fletcher, North Carolina 28732
See Vermont Log Buildings, Inc.

Carroll Homes, Inc.
2434 Forsyth Road,
Orlando, Florida 32807
Products: modified A-frames
Market: Southeast
Literature: brochure, $1

Cathedralite Domes
P. O. Box 880,
Aptos, California 95003
Products: geodesic domes (space frame)
Market: national
Literature: brochure, $3

172

Cedar Forest Products Co.
Polo, Illinois 61064
Products: pre-cut glu-lam timber homes (cedar)
Market: national

Cedar Homes, Inc.
555 116th Avenue N.E.—Suite 150,
Bellevue, Washington 98004
Products: pre-cut solid timber homes (cedar)
Market: far West, Alaska, and Hawaii
Literature: Home Planning Kit, $5

Cluster Shed
   See Timberpeg

Colorado Log Homes
1925 West Dartmouth,
Englewood, Colorado 80033
Products: pre-cut log homes (Engleman spruce)
Market: Central and Western states

Crockett Log Homes, Inc.
Route 9,
West Chesterfield, New Hampshire 03466
Products: pre-cut log homes (hand-peeled pine)
Market: Northeast
Literature: brochure, $2

Deck House, Inc.
930 Main Street,
Acton, Massachusetts 01720
Products: pre-cut package homes
Market: national
Literature: portfolio, $7

Deltec Homes
P. O. Box 6931,
Asheville, North Carolina 28806
Products: panelized polygons and log homes
Market: national
Literature: Poly-Rama planning kit, $3; Log home planning kit, $3

Domes and Homes, Inc.
P. O. Box 365,
Brielle, New Jersey
1605 E. Charleston,
Las Vegas, Nevada 89102
Products: geodesic domes (space frame); panelized octagonal homes
Market: national
Literature: plans catalog, $4

Easy A Division
Southern Structures, Inc.
P. O. Box 52005,
Lafayette, Louisiana 70505
Products: pre-engineered A-frames (steel)
Market: Southern states

Forest Homes, Inc.
P. O. Box 696,
Mesa, Arizona 85201
Products: pre-cut and panelized homes
Market: Southwest

Galaxy Homes, Inc.
1773 Ivy Road,
Oceanside, California 92054
Products: partially prefabricated domes
Market: national

Geodesic Dome Manufacturing Co., Inc.
Box 602,
Plattsburgh, New York 12901
Products: geodesic domes (space frame)
Market: national

Geodesic Domes, Inc.
10290 Davison Road,
Davison, Michigan 48423
Products: geodesic domes (space frame)
Market: national
Literature: floor plans brochure, $1

G. L. Industries, Inc.
999 Newhall Street,
P. O. Box 28130,
San Jose, California 95159
Products: pre-cut and panelized hexagonal homes
Market: far West
Literature: brochure, $3

Green Mountain Cabins, Inc.
Box 190,
Chester, Vermont 05143
Products: pre-cut custom log homes (hand-peeled spruce)
Market: Northeast
Literature: Designing Your Own Green Mountain Log Home, $3.50; Building a Green Mountain Log Cabin, $2.50

Green Mountain Homes
Royalton, Vermont 05068
Products: pre-cut and panelized homes; passive solar homes
Market: national
Literature: plans book, $2.25

Haida Hide, Inc.
19237 Aurora North,
Seattle, Washington 98133
Products: pre-cut and panelized homes
Market: national
Literature: brochures, $3

Herculean Homes Corp.
P. O. Box 357,
Bettendorf, Iowa 52722
Products: pre-cut custom homes
Market: Midwest
Literature: free catalog

Heritage Cedar Homes of New England
Box 250,
North Conway, New Hampshire 03860
Products: pre-cut western red cedar homes
Market: Northeast and Maritime Canada
Literature: brochure, $2

Heritage Homes
4850 Box Elder Street,
Murray, Utah 84107
Products: panelized package homes
Market: national

Hexadome of America
P. O. Box 2351,
La Mesa, California 92041
Products: panelized non-geodesic domes
Market: national
Literature: Send a SASE for information.

International Log Homes Ltd.
P. O. Box 129,
Mill Bay, British Columbia V0R 2P0
Products: pre-cut log homes (fir or cedar)

Justus Company
P. O. Box 98300,
9216 47th Avenue S.W.,
Tacoma, Washington 98499
Products: pre-cut solid timber homes (cedar)
Market: national
Literature: brochure, $4

Kingsberry Homes
61 Perimeter Park,
Atlanta, Georgia 30341
Products: panelized package homes
Market: east of the Rockies
Literature: brochure, $3.50

Lindal Cedar Homes
P. O. Box 24426
Seattle, Washington 98124
Products: pre-cut package homes (western red cedar)
Market: U.S. and Canada
Literature: plans book and design guide, $3

Lodge Logs by MacGregor
P. O. Box 5085,
3200 Gowen Field Road,
Boise, Idaho 83705
Products: pre-cut log homes (lodgepole pine)
Market: Western states
Literature: brochure, $2; construction manual, $5

Logangate Homes
P. O. Box 1855,
3609 Logangate Road,
Youngstown, Ohio 44505
Products: pre-cut and panelized homes
Market: Midwest and Mid-Atlantic states
Literature: portfolio, $3

Lumber Enterprises, Inc.
Star Route—Box 203,
Bozeman, Montana 59715
Products: pre-cut Model-Log homes (lodgepole pine)
Market: national
Literature: catalog, $3

Meyer Round Structures
27649 Industrial Boulevard,
Hayward, California 94545

Products: pre-cut and panelized round houses
Market: far West
Literature: brochure, $2

Miles Homes, Inc.
4500 Lyndale Avenue North,
Minneapolis, Minnesota 55412
Products: pre-cut package homes
Market: east of the Rockies
Literature: Great Homes Idea Book, free

Monterey Domes
P. O. Box 5621-J,
Riverside, California 92517
Products: geodesic domes (hub and strut)
Market: national
Literature: Catalog and Planning Kit, $4; Dome Assembly Manual, $5

National Beauti-Log Cedar Homes, Inc.
1250 South Wilson Way,
Stockton, California 95205
Products: pre-cut log homes (western red cedar)
Market: far West

National Log Construction Co., Inc.
P. O. Box 69,
Thompson Falls, Montana 59873
Products: pre-cut log homes (hollowed pine logs)
Market: national
Literature: plans book, $2.50

New England Log Homes, Inc.
2301 State Street,
P. O. Box 5056
Hamden, Connecticut 06518
Products: pre-cut log homes (hand-peeled plantation pine)
Market: national
Literature: planning kit, $4; construction guide, $15

Northeastern Log Homes, Inc.
Groton, Vermont 05046
Products: pre-cut log homes (eastern white pine)
Market: U.S. and Canada
Literature: brochure, $4

Northern Homes, Inc.
10 LaCrosse Street,
Hudson Falls, New York 12839
Products: pre-cut and panelized package homes
Market: Eastern states
Literature: Portfolio of Homes, $4; Construction Guide, $15

Northern Products, Inc.
Bomarc Road,
Bangor, Maine 04401
Products: pre-cut log homes (eastern white pine)
Market: east of the Rockies
Literature: portfolio, $3

Northwoods Log Homes, Inc.
La Porte, Minnesota 56461
Products: pre-cut custom log homes (western red cedar)
Market: Midwest and Central states

Nor-Wes Cedar Homes
11120 Bridge Road,
Surrey, British Columbia V3V 3T9
Products: pre-cut and panelized homes (cedar)
Market: U.S. and Canada
Literature: catalog, $2.50

Pacific Frontier Homes, Inc.
17975 North Highway 1,
P. O. Box 1247,
Fort Bragg, California 95437
Products: pre-cut package homes
Market: national
Literature: portfolio, $3

Pacific Panel Homes
7951 2nd Avenue South,
Seattle, Washington 98108
Products: panelized package homes
Market: national

Pacific Structures, Inc.
1220 S.W. Morrison Street,
Portland, Oregon 97205
Products: pre-cut custom homes
Market: Pacific Northwest

Pan Abode Cedar Homes
4350 Lake Washington Blvd. North,
Renton, Washington 98055
Products: pre-cut solid timber homes (western red cedar)
Market: U.S. and Canada
Literature: plan book, $7

Pease Company
900 Forest Avenue,
Hamilton, Ohio 45023
Products: pre-cut and panelized homes
Market: Midwest and North Central states
Literature: Pease Book of Homes, $3

Pioneer Log Homes
P. O. Box 267,
Newport, New Hampshire 03773
Products: prefabricated log homes
Market: Northeast
Literature: folder, $3

Polydome, Inc.
1238 Broadway,
El Cajon, California 92021
Products: panelized non-geodesic domes
Market: national
Literature: plans booklet, $2

W. H. Porter, Inc.
P. O. Box 1112-B,
4240 North 136th Avenue,
Holland, Michigan 49423
Products: panelized hexagonal homes

Market: national
Literature: Port-Six Planning Guide, $25

Pre-Cut Timber Homes
P. O. Box 97,
Woodinville, Washington 98072
Products: pre-cut solid timber homes (western red cedar)
Market: national
Literature: plans catalog, $3

President Homes
4808 North Lilac Drive,
Minneapolis, Minnesota 55429
Products: pre-cut custom homes
Market: Midwest and North Central states

Real Log Homes, Inc.
Missoula, Montana 59807
See Vermont Log Buildings, Inc.

Ridge Homes
501 Office Center Drive,
Fort Washington, Pennsylvania 19034
Products: pre-cut custom homes
Market: Eastern states
Literature: Ridge Homes Guide, free

R & L Log Buildings, Inc.
Mt. Upton, New York 13809
Products: pre-cut log homes (red pine)
Market: Northeast
Literature: plans kit, $2

Rondesics Homes Corp.
527 McDowell Street,
Asheville, North Carolina 28803
Products: panelized polygonal homes
Market: east of the Mississippi
Literature: planning kit, $3

Rondo Homes, Inc.
P. O. Box 1679,
Tahoe City, California 95730
Products: pre-cut and panelized 12-sided homes
Market: far West
Literature: brochure, $1

Rustic Log Structures
14000 Interurban Avenue South,
Seattle, Washington 98168
Products: pre-cut custom log homes (hand-peeled lodgepole pine)
Market: Pacific Northwest
Literature: plans book, $4

Serendipity
Pier 9—The Embarcadero,
San Francisco, California 94111
Products: pre-cut package homes
Market: national
Literature: plans book, $5

Shelter Construction and Development Ltd.
R. R. #1,
Glencairn, Ontario L0M 1K0
Products: geodesic dome components

Market: northern U.S. and Canada
Literature: information package, $2

Shelter-Kit, Inc.
Franklin Mills,
Franklin, New Hampshire 03235
Products: pre-engineered modular homes
Market: Northeast
Literature: booklet, $1

Solartran Corporation
Escanaba, Michigan 49829
Products: pre-cut and panelized solar homes
Market: east of the Rockies
Literature: information package, $3.50

Space Structures International Corp.
325 Duffy Avenue,
Hicksville, New York 11801
Products: geodesic domes (hub and strut)
Market: national

Swift Homes
1 Chicago Avenue,
Elizabeth, Pennsylvania 15037
Products: pre-cut and panelized homes
Market: east of the Mississippi
Literature: catalog, $2

Sylvan Products, Inc.
4729 State Highway No. 3, S.W.,
Port Orchard, Washington 98366
Products: pre-cut custom log homes (Douglas fir or pine)
Market: national

Tension Structures, Inc.
9800 Ann Arbor Road,
Plymouth, Michigan 48170
Products: panelized domes (fiberglass)
Market: national

Timber Kit
P. O. Box 704,
Amherst, Massachusetts 01002
Products: pre-cut post and beam homes
Market: national
Literature: brochure, $1

Timberline Company
2015½ Blake Street,
Berkeley, California 94704
Products: geodesic domes (hub and strut)
Market: national
Literature: catalog, $3; planner package, $10

TimberLodge, Inc.
1309 Swift,
North Kansas City, Missouri 64116
Products: pre-cut redwood homes
Market: national
Literature: planning kit, $3

Timberpeg
Box 1358,
Claremont, New Hampshire 03743
Products: pre-cut package homes
Market: national
Literature: design portfolio, $5

Topsider Vacation Homes
Carter Construction & Engineering Co., Inc.
P. O. Box 849,
Yadkinville, North Carolina 27055
Products: pre-cut and panelized octagonal homes
Market: national
Literature: planning package, $3

True-Craft Log Structures Ltd.
60 Riverside Drive,
North Vancouver, British Columbia V7H 1T4
Products: pre-cut log homes
Market: U.S. and Canada
Literature: catalog, $2

Vacation Land Homes, Inc.
P. O. Box 292,
Bellaire, Michigan 49615
Products: panelized package homes
Market: national
Literature: catalog, $3

Vermont Log Buildings, Inc.
Hartland, Vermont 05048
Products: pre-cut log homes (pine)
Market: national
Literature: Real Log Homes catalog, $5

Ward Cabin Company
Box 72,
Houlton, Maine 04730
Products: pre-cut log homes (northern white cedar)
Market: east of the Mississippi
Literature: brochure, $5

Well-Built Homes
Route #22,
Bridgewater, New Jersey 08807
Products: erected shell homes
Market: Mid-Atlantic states

Western Valley Log Homes
P. O. Box 254,
Victor, Montana 59875
Products: pre-cut log homes
Market: Central and Western states
Literature: catalog, $3.50; construction manual, $15

Wickes Lumber
515 North Washington Avenue,
Saginaw, Michigan 48607
Products: panelized package homes
Market: national

Wilderness Log Homes
R. R. 2,
Plymouth, Wisconsin 53073
Products: pre-cut log homes (cedar or pine)
Market: national
Literature: plans book, $3.50

Yankee Barn Homes
Drawer A,
Grantham, New Hampshire 03753
Products: pre-cut and panelized barn homes
Market: east of the Rockies
Literature: planning package, $4

Youngstrom Log Homes
Box 385,
Blackfoot, Idaho 83221
Products: pre-cut log homes (lodgepole pine)
Market: Western states
Literature: brochure, $2

# Quick Indexes

### A-Frames
Bellaire Log Cabin Manufacturing Co., 172
Carroll Homes, Inc., 172
Easy A, 74, 173
Forest Homes, Inc., 70, 173
Herculean Homes Corp., 173
Pacific Panel Homes, 174
Serendipity, 174
Swift Homes, 175
TimberLodge, Inc., 68-69, 175
Vacation Land Homes, Inc., 72, 175

### Chalets
Alta Industries Ltd., 172
American Timber Homes, Inc., 172
L. C. Andrew, Inc., 172
Cedar Homes, Inc., 82-83, 173
Haida Hide, Inc., 173
Heritage Homes, 173
Justus Company, 80-81, 173
Lindal Cedar Homes, 78-79, 173
Northern Products, Inc., 174
Nor-Wes Cedar Homes, 174
Pacific Frontier Homes, Inc., 174
Pacific Structures, Inc., 174
Pan Abode Cedar Homes, 84-85, 174
Pre-Cut Timber Homes, 174
Vacation Land Homes, Inc., 175
Vermont Log Buildings, Inc., 175
Ward Cabin Company, 175
Wickes Lumber, 86, 175

### Contemporaries
Acorn Structures, Inc., 128-29, 172
Blackstock Homes, 172
Capp Homes, 172
Cedar Homes, Inc., 173
Deck House, Inc., 136-37, 173
Green Mountain Homes, 173
Kingsberry Homes, 126-27, 173
Lindal Cedar Homes, 132, 173
Logangate Homes, 173
Northern Homes, Inc., 174
Pacific Frontier Homes, Inc., 130-31, 174
Pacific Panel Homes, 174
Pacific Structures, Inc., 174
Pan Abode Cedar Homes, 174
Pease Company, 138, 174
Pre-Cut Timber Homes, 134-35, 174
Ridge Homes, 174
Serendipity, 174
Swift Homes, 175
Timber Kit, 175
Timberpeg, 175
Vacation Land Homes, Inc., 133, 175

### Domes
American Geodesic, Inc., 60-61, 172
The Big Outdoors People, Inc., 54-55, 172
Cathedralite Domes, 52-53, 173
Domes and Homes, Inc., 173
Galaxy Homes, Inc., 62, 173
Geodesic Dome Manufacturing Co., Inc., 56-57, 173
Geodesic Domes, Inc., 173
Hexadome of America, 173
Monterey Domes, 50-51, 174
Polydome, Inc., 174
Shelter Construction and Development Ltd., 58, 174-75
Space Structures International Corp., 175
Tension Structures, Inc., 64, 175
Timberline Company, 175

### Hideaways and Starters
Air-Lock Log Co., Inc., 172
American Pioneer Buildings, Inc., 172
L. C. Andrew, Inc., 172
Authentic Homes Corp., 172
Bellaire Log Cabin Manufacturing Co., 172
National Log Construction Co., Inc., 174
Pacific Frontier Homes, Inc., 174
Pan Abode Cedar Homes, 174
Pre-Cut Timber Homes, 146, 174
Shelter-Kit, Inc., 142-43, 175
Timberpeg, 144, 175
Wilderness Log Homes, 175

### Log Houses
Air-Lock Log Co., Inc., 32-33, 172
Alta Industries, Ltd., 38, 172
American Pioneer Buildings, Inc., 42, 172
L. C. Andrew, Inc., 36-37, 172
Arkansas Log Homes, Inc., 172
Authentic Homes Corp., 18-19, 172
Beaver Log Homes, 44, 172
Bellaire Log Cabin Manufacturing Co., 172
Boyne Falls Log Homes, 24-25, 172
Building Logs, Inc., 172
Can-Am Log Houses Ltd., 172
Carolina Log Buildings, Inc., 172
Colorado Log Homes, 173
Crockett Log Homes, Inc., 173
Deltec Homes, 173
Green Mountain Cabins, Inc., 173
International Log Homes Ltd., 173
Lodge Logs by MacGregor, 173
Lumber Enterprises, Inc., 173
National Beauti-Log Cedar Homes, Inc., 174
National Log Construction Co., Inc., 32-33, 174
New England Log Homes, Inc., 26-27, 174
Northeastern Log Homes, Inc., 34, 174
Northern Products, Inc., 174
Northwoods Log Homes, Inc., 174
Pioneer Log Homes, 174
Real Log Homes, Inc., 22-23, 174
R & L Log Buildings, Inc., 174
Rustic Log Structures, 29-30, 174
Sylvan Products, Inc., 175
True-Craft Log Structures Ltd., 175
Vermont Log Buildings, Inc., 175
Ward Cabin Company, 40-41, 175
Western Valley Log Homes, 175
Wilderness Log Homes, 175
Youngstrom Log Homes, 175

### Polygons and Round Houses
AGI: The Shelter People, 172
Air-Lock Log Co., Inc., 172
American Timber Homes, Inc., 172
Authentic Homes Corp., 172
Cedar Homes, Inc., 173
Deltec Homes, 173
Domes and Homes, Inc., 173
Forest Homes, Inc., 173
G. L. Industries, 102, 173
Lindal Cedar Homes, 173
Lodge Logs by MacGregor, 173
Meyer Round Structures, 100, 173-74
National Log Construction Co., Inc., 174
Pacific Panel Homes, 174
W. H. Porter, Inc., 98-99, 174
Rondesics Homes Corp., 95-96, 174
Rondo Homes, Inc., 174
Topsider Vacation Homes, 92-93, 175

### Solar Houses
Acorn Structures, Inc., 154-55, 172
Green Mountain Homes, 152-53, 173
Lodge Logs by MacGregor, 148, 173
Monterey Domes, 148, 174
Solartran Corporation, 150-51, 175

### Traditionals
The Aladdin Company, 172
American Timber Homes, Inc., 114-15, 172
Blackstock Homes, 172
Capp Homes, 118-19, 172
Cedar Forest Products Co., 120, 173
Forest Homes, Inc., 173
Haida Hide, Inc., 122, 173
Herculean Homes Corp., 173
Heritage Cedar Homes of New England, 173
Heritage Homes, 173
Kingsberry Homes, 173
Miles Homes, Inc., 116-17, 174
Northern Homes, Inc., 110-11, 174
Pacific Panel Homes, 174
Pease Company, 174
Pre-Cut Timber Homes, 174
President Homes, 174
Ridge Homes, 119, 174
Swift Homes, 175
TimberLodge, Inc., 175
Timberpeg, 112-13, 175
Well-Built Homes, 175
Wickes Lumber, 175
Yankee Barn Homes, 175